# KYLIE NAKED

## A BIOGRAPHY

# KYLIE NAKED
## A BIOGRAPHY

Jenny Stanley-Clarke and Nigel Goodall

EBURY
PRESS

20075441

'I don't have to try to be a sex bomb, I am one!'
*Kylie Minogue*

First published in the UK in 2002

© Jenny Stanley-Clarke & Nigel Goodall 2002

1 3 5 7 9 10 8 6 4 2

Jenny Stanley-Clarke and Nigel Goodall have asserted their right to be identified
as authors of this work under the Copyright, Designs and Patents Act 1988

Ebury Press
Random House, 20 Vauxhall Bridge Road, London SW1V 2SA

Random House Australia Pty Limited
20 Alfred Street, Milsons Point, Sydney, New South Wales 2061, Australia

Random House New Zealand Limited
18 Poland Road, Glenfield, Auckland 10, New Zealand

Random House (Pty) Limited
Endulini, 5A Jubilee Road, Parktown 2193, South Africa

The Random House Group Limited Reg. No. 954009

A CIP catalogue record for this book is available from the British Library

ISBN: 0091880963

Jacket design by the Senate

Printed and bound in Great Britain by Mackays of Chatham plc

Papers used by Ebury Press are natural, recyclable products
made from wood grown in sustainable forests.

# CONTENTS

*To our respective children, Daniel, Ben, Adam and Kim*

# ACKNOWLEDGEMENTS

There are no people more important to a non-fiction writer than sources. In addition to those listed in that section of this book we wish to thank all those who helped with this book for their support, encouragement and inspiration.

We are hugely indebted to Neil Rees of LiMBO Kylie Minogue Online (www.kylie.co.uk) and Andrew Cowan-Martin, former head of management at PWL, for sharing their astute knowledge and expertise with us, especially Neil for helping out with the discography and for generously making available exclusive interview material and other information. And of course, everyone at Ebury Press.

We would also like to thank Kylie herself, whose career and public profile for more than half her life inspired us to write this book in the first place. We hope she and her manager Terry Blamey discover that her inspiration has been rewarded with a book that accurately and fairly sums up her life so far.

# INTRODUCTION

Whenever people discover we have written this book, we're bombarded with questions. What is Kylie like? How was it to meet her? Is she really that tiny? When did you last interview her? And if you interview her again can we come along? We would, of course, have preferred to ask Kylie if she would be interested in co-operating with an authorised biography to coincide with her massive arena tour of the UK and Europe in April 2002 but, inevitably, there was no time to do so.

Our intent has been to present a sensitive and truthful account of Kylie Minogue as a tribute to her and her legion of fans – which includes ourselves. Those who have met her tend to mention that barefoot she stands a little over five feet, but far more important is the fact that Kylie at 33 is truly a phenomenon who holds a unique position in the music world. With almost 15 years behind her as a significant recording artist and more than 20 as an accomplished actress, she is in the enviable position of being able to compete both commercially and critically with every one of her musical peers, both male and female.

Kylie is the comeback queen who never went away. Through her own desire to progress, improve and re-invent, she has made herself irreplaceable. She remains untainted and as fresh as the day she first stepped into the spotlight, but with more drive and ambition than ever before.

To date she has released eight studio albums, six long-play videos, greatest hits and live packages, a multitude of other hits and remix compilations, and 38 hit singles throughout the world, many of which are regarded as pop classics. One of her most recent singles, 'Can't Get You Out Of My Head', ended up as *the* Number One record in almost every territory in which it was released. Not only that but it has sold literally in its millions, and looks very likely to repeat the same success across America in 2002. And the album *Fever*, from which the single was taken, has enjoyed the same success, both here in Britain and throughout the world.

Add to this her successful roles on both television and movie screen, and you have a rollercoaster ride of a career. Today Kylie could not be more successful if she tried. At long last, talent has won through, and almost miraculously she has gained the credit and critical acclaim that has for so long evaded her.

Looking back to June 1991, following the release of her 13th single, 'Shocked', the British music industry bible *Music Week* declared what a musical force Kylie had become. The only act in the history of British popular music to have had her first 13 releases all go Top Ten. She has now had 31 consecutive hits in Britain, and 38 worldwide, 21 of which have reached the Top Ten, and six of those reaching Number One.

Kylie has become one of the world's most successful female musical artists, but it was not quite as simple as that in the beginning. Having more or less grown up in front of the television cameras since the age of 11, she has managed to maintain the integrity with which she entered show business. The first of her acting roles was in the Australian television drama series *The Sullivans*, followed by other popular dramas such as *Skyways, Zoo Family* and *The Henderson Kids*. Soon after her 17th birthday, when Kylie left school to pursue a career in acting, she landed the role of Charlene Mitchell in *Neighbours*. To this day she is one of the most popular characters to come out of that Australian television series.

Although she has never known the troubled years of so many other young hopefuls, auditioning by day, waiting tables by night and going wild with excitement every time some half interested person recognises them from a commercial, paradoxically she never wanted to be famous when she was a child. If anything, it happened purely by accident. If her fame wasn't exactly handed to her on a plate, it was at least delivered to her door.

By the time she was out of her teens she had, after all, won five Logie awards (the Australian equivalent of an Emmy), and was the youngest actress ever to achieve such an honour. In 1987 she won the Silver Logie for 'Most Popular Actress' and in 1988 she was the first artist ever to win four Logies on one night, including the Gold for 'Most Popular Personality on Australian Television' and another Silver.

Within two years, Kylie was performing as adeptly on the big screen as she had in any television drama when her first feature film, *The Delinquents*, was released around the world to rave reviews. By December of that year it had become the Christmas blockbuster, hurtling Kylie into the limelight once more.

By that time, Kylie was a household name throughout the world, with a whole generation of children being named after her. When Kylie's *Greatest Hits* was released in 1992 debuting at Number One on the album chart, going gold on release and accompanied by an equally successful Number One video, she had also been the guest of royalty, both in Britain and Europe and a favourite of several invitations for Royal Command Performances. Perhaps that is why her fans, not content with merely labelling her as their own version of royalty, have crowned her the goddess, or at other times, the princess of pop.

With five sell-out world tours, she established herself as a live performer of incredible calibre with notable and critically acclaimed performances at the Lennon Memorial Concert in Liverpool in 1992, opening Mushroom Records' 25th Anniversary Concert and the new Fox Studios complex in 1998, both in Melbourne, the Paraolympics in 2000 and, of course, stunning the world as the queen of showgirls in front of four billion people at the closing ceremony of the Sydney Olympics in the same year. We were particularly captivated when we watched her on *An Audience With* and *Live in Sydney*.

But take away the feathers, the stiletto heels and the familiar disproportionate smile, and look a little deeper and you will discover that despite the fame, fortune and millions of records and concert tickets sold, such figures and awards are irrelevant. Ask her, and you will quickly discover that she has little idea of how many records she has sold (now rapidly approaching 50 million), how many awards she has won or even how many years she has been doing all this for.

Her drive to perform is as instinctive as it's ever been; her performance and fame amazingly free from ego. Even more important is the fact that, because of her strong and endearing personality, she has made herself many things to many people and, in doing so, has cornered the market for simply making folk happy. The media are fascinated by her, the industry applauds her and her fans adore her. She is a unique icon of her own making.

Sharing an emotional bond she has with fans, whom she openly and fondly regards as if they were members of her own family, and with those she meets on her career journey, she has guaranteed herself a permanent place in our lives. Whether Cute, Sex, Dance or IndieKylie, on the radio, television, stage or silver screen, she plays out the roles she is to many people. But most of all, she is adored for simply being Kylie.

Having written about her life and her career, we intend to share with others the opportunity to witness her entrancing quality. Whether at Wembley, Manchester or Birmingham, we wouldn't miss it for the world.

See you on the tour!

# ONE

# KYLIE FEVER

It's twenty past three in the morning, and Kylie Minogue is crying. She's crying because she is tired. And all she wants to do is go to bed and sleep. She tried earlier, about an hour or so before but her mind was racing. Now she's up, out of bed and in the kitchen of the pad she once shared with a girlfriend, not far from Parlophone, the record label she's currently signed to. The same one The Beatles made so famous. She flicks through the newspaper on the table until she calms down and can go back to bed.

She has every reason to want a good night's sleep, rather than the exhaustion she now faces trying to get to the end of another day. From tomorrow, though, after one more interview with another magazine, another journalist and another photo-shoot, she has five days off from the most successful year of her career.

That undoubted year of Kylie, as journalist Simon Gage correctly tagged it, had kicked off as early as January when she went back into several studios with numerous producers and engineers to start work on recording a follow-up album to *Light*

*Years* that would build on the success of that album from the
previous year. This time there would be more songs to choose
from simply because publishers no longer had her pegged as an
indie singer.

It wouldn't matter. As with *Light Years* the choices would
feature a number of her own writing and production collaborations
anyway. Although not planned as such, there would be 12 songs but
now with a more contemporary production than she had previously known. It would not, however, prove an easy task by any
means as all the material would have to be written and recorded
before she got into rehearsals for her then upcoming tour of the UK
and Australia in just two months' time. Otherwise it would simply
be a case of using any free days she had on the tour to spend either
co-writing or recording. And if that wasn't possible, then she would
just have to wait until later in the year to complete the tracks. And
to all intents and purposes that's what she did.

But the hectic schedule of touring and everything else going
on in her life would leave her completely worn out by the time she
returned to the studios later that summer.

'I'm totally shattered,' she said at the time. 'Everything has
been so crazy. I've been trying to get my act together, but I am so
exhausted I can barely string a sentence together. Making this
album has really taken its toll.'

She didn't let it show though. Even if she did find a break in
her schedule, she seemed to have filled it with work, work, work.
She launched her own range of lingerie in Australia, at
Melbourne's Fashion Week. 'They were gonna be called Lucky
Knickers,' she explained. 'But it turns out the name Lucky is
owned for everything, so we're not actually allowed to call them
that any more. So now they're called LoveKylie knickers. But we
still call them Lucky Knickers.'

As if that wasn't enough, she even found time to appear in Baz Luhrmann's *Moulin Rouge*. 'I play the green fairy in it,' she said thrilled. 'I have boundless amounts of respect for Baz Luhrmann.' She admits to having made some odd choices in her previous films. 'I firmly believe that I need the right person to help me reach my potential. With acting, I'm not an overly confident person, although I have to act most days with what I do. There's performance on different levels, but they're all versions of me.'

She had even cut a version in Sydney of Olivia Newton-John's 1981 hit 'Physical', written by Steve Kipner and Terry Shaddick, for the soundtrack, much the same as the slow bluesy treatment she would later perform on the tour. Not that it would end up in the movie or for that matter elsewhere, aside from the Australian *Light Years: Limited Edition Tour Pack*. Perhaps like the original it was considered too raunchy for its sexual innuendo.

Twenty years earlier Newton-John's version had been banned by most radio stations for that very reason, even if it did, at the time, become the equal second-longest chart-topper in US pop history behind Elvis Presley's 'Hound Dog'. Like Kylie's 'Spinning Around', it was 'Physical' that took Olivia's image from wholesome girl-next-door to her 1980s raunchy persona.

If nothing else, it demonstrates Kylie's impeccable taste for good song material, whether original or cover. Although rumours still persist that Kylie and Olivia are to record a duet together, it is something that they still have to do.

Even when she did resume recording after the tour and was thinking that she had finished the album, with 13 tracks in the can, she received another song, 'Come Into My World', from Rob Davis and Cathy Dennis, the writing team of 'Can't Get You Out Of My Head'.

The song made such an impression that she immediately booked more studio time that evening, recorded the song that night and added it the following day to the album that was to be called *Fever*. At the same time though, she removed two other tracks. 'Whenever You Feel Like It' was originally intended for *Light Years* but held over for use elsewhere, but still to this day has not been issued; likewise 'Good Like That' remains unreleased apart from in Japan, although by February 2002 it would also turn up in the UK – on CD 1 of her then newest single, 'In Your Eyes'.

Although she had played three gigs at Shepherds Bush three years earlier, it would be her first tour of the UK in ten years. Never one for a minimalist approach, in her production ideas for the tour she would build the shows on the theatrical extravaganza she had devised for her tours in previous years. This would, of course, incorporate living out the dream of her showgirl, cabaret and pop fantasies. It would also spell out indulgence.

She wanted her audience 'to have fun, take a journey through the years. The concert will have a mixture of old and new and will have quite a musical feel. To create a sort of storyline to which the songs can be related. Let's say pop, cabaret and disco – and whatever else takes shape. It's a luxury now to have such a history with my audience. We've grown up together and have a lot to share in the show.'

By the time tickets went on sale the previous November the tour was now called On a Night Like This 2001. And when rehearsals began shortly after laying down the first tracks for the *Fever* album, she had put together a main show set list, encore numbers, and even ones that would be omitted or added to some of the European dates. One of those included everywhere was the debut of 'Can't Get You Out Of My Head'. First put down at the studio sessions in January, it seemed unlikely that it would ever turn up on a single and perhaps even less likely to be the monster hit it eventually became. To this day it is the best-selling single of her career and the most played record of all time on UK radio.

But maybe it's what keeps Kylie on the ball. It wasn't just the 12,000 or more fans at each concert who by now were probably expecting an event rather than a show, but the complexity of what she was planning to do on stage: working with eight dancers, singing 22 songs, making five costume changes and moving in style from Seventies kitsch to current high-tech pop while everything is recorded and filmed at the end of the tour. No wonder she was feeling exhausted backstage just before show-time at the Sydney Entertainment Centre.

All the same, the reviews were ecstatic. 'If her sell-out concerts and stunning performances are any measure, Kylie's pop crown looks safe for years to come,' said the *Sunday Mirror*. Such choruses of approval were echoed by the *Daily Telegraph*:

> Sold out nights such as this must be sweet revenge for Kylie Minogue, the actress-turned singer who has been a feature at the top end of the British charts over three decades. From the opening note to the thankyous to her dancers and band, the key to Kylie's pop longevity, her adorability never once faltered.

*The Independent* agreed:

> As well as a formidable singing voice, she has a person-ality all her own and it shines best amid hi-NRG beats, silver tassels and six inch stiletto heels ... it's riotous fun ... a fantastic encore ... has the audience screaming themselves silly.

It was much the same elsewhere, noted the *Daily Mail*:

> To the delight of the screaming crowd she sings her latest hits, including her number one single *Spinning Around*. It's an intoxicating mix of pop, cabaret, camp, glitz and glamour and an adoring crowd – excited teenage girls, couples and throngs of gay men – laps up every single foot-tapping minute of it. Kylie is in her element, revelling in her status as the queen of pop – a woman at the apex of her career.

Even the *NME* joined in the applause:

> Tonight's show scales heights of theatrical aceness... Generation K has glimpsed heaven. And, that is just slightly wonderful.

The reviews couldn't have been better if Kylie had written them herself. And having won one victory, she prepared herself for another. Adding an unprecedented number of extra dates to another arena tour in the UK for the following year, after initial dates had sold out within one hour, the total number of ticket sales that October had now easily eclipsed Madonna's Drowned World tour. Not only that but she was also breaking other box-office standards. Over one weekend she sold more than 140,000 tickets. At the Newcastle Telewest venue, tickets sold so fast that she broke the previous record set by Robbie Williams. It was clear that Kylie's next outing around Britain and Europe was already the most popular tour since God knows when.

She celebrated this with the release of a new single. 'Can't Get You Out Of My Head', the song Kylie had premiered on the tour earlier in the year, was released on 17 September. According to Parlophone's press release, the track would display a harder sound than had been featured previously on the now platinum-selling *Light Years* and the three singles that came off that album. Two months earlier, of course, the writing was on the wall. A 12-inch promo featuring a Superchumbo mix of the track had, by that time, already been going down a storm in clubs.

In the video, directed by Kylie's favourite video maker Dawn Shadforth, Kylie would once again demonstrate just how impeccable her taste can be. First shown on *CD:UK* two weeks earlier, the promo remains among the best loved of all Kylie's videos, and would even go on to be voted and win the Best Video in *Heat* magazine's readers' poll. It also won in the Best Outfit category.

Not surprising really when you consider that the white hooded catsuit she wore among other costumes in the urban environment setting of the piece was probably more skimpy and designer show-stopping than anything she had sported previously. Slashed to expose part of her bare breasts down to her naval and again up each side of her legs to her thighs, with just a hint of her naked bottom every time she moved, it was indeed a masterpiece. Even with the help of double-sided toupé tape to keep her nipples covered, as was to be the case for the later 'In Your Eyes' video, it was still a wonder how she managed to keep everything just about covered.

But according to Kylie, 'All that vampy stuff had been brewing in my head and it just reached the point where I had to let it out. I was just so tired of flashing the pearly whites and feeling like I was the star of a soap commercial.'

As if to aid her never-ending quest to be gracious, Kylie remembers the moment when she discovered that her single was

due out the same day as Victoria Beckham's first solo effort, 'Not
Such An Innocent Girl'.

'I rang my manager as soon as I heard and asked whether
we should change the date but it would have been a nightmare.
Also, I'd just be up against someone else,' she says. 'The cards
had been dealt and I just thought I should play the game and go
along with it.'

She need not have worried. 'Can't Get You Out Of My Head',
quite remarkably, outsold the Beckham single eight to one.

Within a week of the release of 'Can't Get You Out Of My Head',
Kylie was filming *An Audience with Kylie Minogue* in front of the
television cameras. The day she recorded the programme, in the
same format that previous performers such as Tom Jones and
Cliff Richard had done before her, on Sunday, 23 September for
broadcast two weeks later, the single had entered the UK charts
at Number One.

Kylie couldn't believe it either. It was just incredible, she told
*Heat* magazine when they caught up with her for a December
2001 feature. She was rehearsing for the TV show that morning
when she heard the news. 'My record company has a number you
can call which gives the week's chart result; my TV promo lady
handed me the phone and the voice on the phone was saying,
"Kylie's entered at Number One with sales of 306,000 copies,"
and it was like a movie moment. I couldn't speak and I just
handed her the phone and said, "You have to listen because that
can't be right." I was just flabbergasted.'

Her delight was as evident as that of the celebrity guests,
colleagues, friends and family who crowded into the London
Studios that Sunday evening to watch Kylie belt out a selection of
her greatest hits, some newer material from the then forthcoming

album and to take centre stage in between the music to answer questions from a star-studded audience including Boy George, Julian Clary, Pete Waterman, Cat Deeley, Lady Victoria Hervey, cast members of *Coronation Street*, *EastEnders* and *Brookside*, her brother and sister, Brendan and Dannii; and, of course, Anne Charleston, her former on-screen mother from *Neighbours*.

Not only did she dazzle the audience with her eye-catching and stunning costume changes during the taping of the show, but she was also able to spring a series of surprises on them. One of which was inviting Olympic boxing gold medallist Audley Harrison, *Big Brother's* Paul Clarke and *Brookside* star Phil Olivier up on to the stage to join her in a spirited rendition of her first-ever hit 'The Locomotion'.

Another, of course, was the duet she performed with Kermit the Frog on 'Especially For You', the Number One hit she had originally shared with Jason Donovan in 1989. And as if that wasn't enough to strike a chord with the crowds both in the studio and at home, then the toe-tap collaboration with Adam Garcia on 'Better The Devil You Know' certainly did. It was quite simply a superbly executed song and dance routine, reminiscent of classic Hollywood.

The album *Fever* was released just two days after the 60-minute special had aired on ITV 1. It featured Kylie on the cover standing sideways against a white studio wall, holding a microphone not far above her head, arms stretched, and the microphone cable running down the length of her body into a heap on the floor. She is in a white T-shirt, matching laced knickers with an extended tie-up sash hanging down over her bare slightly tilted legs to just below the back of her knees, and on her feet, white stiletto heels. Even if it hadn't had the words *Kylie* and *Fever* on the top left and bottom right corners, it would still have been perfect.

Parlophone was excited by the album and promoted it heavily, printing up the usual point-of-sale material, placing ads in all the regular magazines and newspapers, and even launching an exclusive online behind-the-scenes series of short programmes entitled 'Feel The Fever' on Kylie's official website. It would track her through the various stages of the campaign for the album and include candid footage shot at photo sessions and video shoots, rehearsals and interviews, with Kylie herself providing commentary. Although she would never be taken up by some quarters of the music fraternity, it was suddenly okay to admit to liking Kylie Minogue.

Reviewing the album, *NME* came to a clear conclusion:

in many ways it's her most daring yet, if not her best. Relentlessly upbeat, some songs nonetheless take a few listens until they make sense, but 'Can't Get You Out of My Head' took most people a few listens to get their heads around and now it's being hailed as one of Kylie's best ever singles! There are plenty of potential singles to choose from on this album and if you think the country was taken over by *Light Years* just wait for Kylie Fever to begin!

Certainly it already had, and it didn't go unnoticed either in the plethora of award shows with which the music industry now seems to abound. Not for the first time in her career, following similar nominations elsewhere, Kylie would scoop the Best Tour and Best Single awards at the *Top of the Pops* ceremony, Best Female Artist at the ARIA awards in Australia and Best Comeback at the Bambi's in Germany. A clear favourite in many people's eyes, it didn't seem feasible that 'Can't Get You Out Of

My Head' only made it to third place in ITV 1's *Record of the Year*. And her show-stopping performances at MTV Europe's music awards and the *Smash Hits* readers' poll party were far greater than any award could have possibly earned her.

All in all, it truly had been her most successful year. Even if, as she sat in a makeup chair in a tiny West London studio having blonde extensions woven into her hair and preparing for the first of two days' filming for her next video 'In Your Eyes', she must have already been looking back in reflective mood.

'Yeah definitely. It's been an insane year,' she laughs. 'It's funny because people are all saying, "Oh, you must be so happy, it's been such a great year." I don't know if happy is exactly the word, because it has involved an incredible amount of hard work and I think the moments of happiness are short-lived. I haven't really had much time to stop and enjoy it.'

## TWO

**MAY 1968 – MAY 1985**

# JUST A GIRL FROM MELBOURNE

Every new mother, quite naturally, harbours dreams for her child. In her eyes, no baby is going to be as special as the one to whom she has just given birth. Nor as intelligent, talented or as extraordinarily beautiful as her own. As far as any mother is concerned, every tiny, vulnerable part of their offspring, laying sound asleep in the neo-natal ward, is destined for some kind of greatness.

Carol Jones, born and raised in Wales, could not be certain of that. Just four years after she had married, then barely twenty, and moved south from Queensland, she presented her husband, Ron Minogue, a native Australian, with their first-born daughter. Much to their delight, Kylie Ann, named after the Australian word for 'boomerang', was born on 28 May 1968 at Bethlehem Hospital in Melbourne. But never, not even in her wildest dreams, could she or Ron, have imagined the kind of phenome-non that their little girl would become.

Kylie, however, didn't remain Ron and Carol's only child for long. Two years later in 1970, when Kylie was two, Brendan, their only son, was born, and a year after that, their second daughter, Danielle, or Dannii for short.

Kylie, Brendan and Dannii spent most of their early child-hood moving from house to house, school to school, and town to town. Right up to the time when Kylie was 12, the family seemed to have moved around Melbourne as regular as clockwork, rarely staying put for more than a few years at a time. An existence that young Kylie disliked intensely. In fact, she hated it. From her point of view, it was quite understandable. No sooner had she made new friends and settled into a new school than the packing boxes came out again and the removal vans ferried them to a new street and another new home.

In fact, it wasn't until 1980 that Ron, a qualified accountant, found the job he had been seeking for some time, in the accounts department of a local council. So idyllic was the opportunity that it convinced him the time was ripe to move his family yet again. It was also a time to take another step forward into the lifestyle that he had worked so hard towards. Now the Minogues could finally settle into their new home in the serene Surrey Hills area without fear of further upheaval.

Their new home was, in many ways, a move to more modern luxuries than they had previously known. For Kylie, Brendan and Dannii, a room each of their own. If that was something that had escaped them until now, probably with Kylie and Dannii sharing, they could at last have the independence they craved.

As if that were not enough, there was a spacious garden for outdoor play where Ron and Carol could enjoy the same unfettered liberty as the children for relaxation and some gardening, if they wished. What's more, the red-bricked house was also situated close to Camberwell High School for Kylie to enrol as a first-year pupil.

Many journalists have noted the astonishing, almost uncanny, resemblance their new neighbourhood bore to that of Ramsay Street – another neighbourhood that in the years ahead would become Kylie's second home for a time and, more importantly, Australia's favourite community for television viewers around the world.

Again, Kylie hated it. As before, she had to leave friends, schools and familiar hangouts behind. All she could do was grit her teeth and bear it. It probably helped that she had other things on her mind. One of those other things, she discovered, was acting. Singing was another.

'When I was eight,' Kylie recalls, 'my pals and I went up to my bedroom, put on our party frocks and mimed to Abba records using broom handles as microphones.'

But it was at the tender and impressionable age of ten that Kylie experienced an apotheosis that was to inspire her deeply and which, to some extent, would reverberate through the rest of her life. It occurred during the 110 minutes in which she sat watching Robert Stigwood and Allan Carr's 1977 film version of the musical *Grease*.

It was the penultimate scene of the movie that had her spellbound. The one in which Sandy, played by another Australian export, Olivia Newton-John, changes from the diffident adolescent in plain frocks and ponytail she has played throughout the film, into a knowing, confident young woman decked out in black leather. Like all those other young girls,

Kylie too wanted to be Sandy – or, more to the point, she wanted to be Olivia in performance alongside John Travolta on 'You're The One That I Want'.

Kylie was quite captivated with the idea of this transformation and, like Sandy, she would effect a series of similar metamorphoses throughout her future career.

Of course the difference between Kylie and all those other young girls, who no doubt had played out the scene in front of their bedroom mirror, singing into a hairbrush as if it were a microphone while the hit record played over and over on the stereo, was that Kylie got the chance to do it for real and even to overshadow the enormous success Newton-John achieved.

And by a pure stroke of irony, Kylie has her younger sister Dannii to thank for the opportunity.

Kylie's aunt Suzette was attached to the acting profession, and after learning of a small role for a youngster in the cast of *The Sullivans*, then Australia's popular World War II television soap, she immediately thought of her young niece. Not Kylie, but Dannii, the stage-struck member of the family, then just nine years old, with an almost obsessive intensity for performing.

For the audition, Dannii had persuaded Carol to go with her. And Carol in turn, a one-time ballerina whose dancing shoes she had long hung up, convinced them to allow sister Kylie to go with them. As soon as she set foot inside the television studio, the casting director set his eyes on her, and immediately knew his search for the right girl had ended then and there.

'They were trying to find someone for a role in *The Sullivans*,' recalls Kylie, 'which, of course, we all grew up with. They asked if my sister could go in, and of course my mother said, "Well, can I bring both girls in, I don't want any bickering or anything." So we both went in and I got that role.'

Dannii was simply aghast with this sudden turn of events and, despite Carol's attempts to pour oil over troubled waters and convince her younger daughter that she should be pleased for the older and more experienced Kylie, the damage had already been done, hadn't it? Nothing it seemed, could prevent the seeds of sibling rivalry that, according to some observers, were now clearly sown. But today, both girls are quick to sweep such accusations aside. If anything, they laugh about the speculation.

The part in question was that of Carla, a Dutch war orphan who becomes friendly with a bunch of Australian soldiers. If Kylie's only memory of her on-screen debut was the Dutch accent that she wasn't very good at, criticising her when she was so young and so inexperienced because she couldn't imitate the native tongue of her character is like damning Rembrandt because he painted one nostril larger than the other. It simply didn't matter at that stage of her career. Even if no one could buy her Australian-tinged tone wrapped around the correct accent of a Dutch girl, was it really that important? After all, a few episodes later, she would be killed off anyway.

Even more ironic than that, however, was Dannii's role in the soap soon after Kylie had shot her final scenes. She appeared, albeit briefly, as a girl who claimed to be Carla. With the obvious resemblance to her sister, the choice to cast her in that role was indeed a good one.

It didn't matter to Kylie. By then she had moved on to her second acting role as a cantankerous kid called Robin for one episode of *Skyways*, another popular Australian soap based in an airport. Although she may have seen the role as a deliberate attempt at an acting career, she would most probably admit today that *The Sullivans* was nothing more than an accidental slice of fun, despite the fact that she was still very young.

It was during the filming of the one episode of *Skyways* in which she had been hired to appear that she would meet Jason Donovan for the first time, cast in the part of her brother. Jason was then much younger and chubbier than the heartthrob everyone, including Kylie, would come to love and adore. 'He had his chubby face and little bowl haircut, and I had big buck teeth and long blonde hair,' Kylie laughs. 'We have this plane crash. It was really awful, but a good start.'

After that, Kylie did not work again in front of the cameras for at least another four years. Instead she picked up the threads of a normal childhood with a new school and new friends, not once giving her acting career another mention. Well, not until that supposed sister rivalry surfaced once again. Only this time, it was Dannii who was in the spotlight, and gaining far more attention than Kylie had earned from her first two acting roles.

Dannii's regular television appearance on *Young Talent Time* had bestowed on her a kind of celebrity – not surprising really when you consider that the weekly variety programme was among the most watched in Australia at that time. And that alone left Kylie out in the cold.

Charged with the task of helping to deal with the mountain of fan mail that seemed to drift in at a steady rate, Kylie quickly discovered she was no longer a person in her own right. Neither did she have her own identity.

Formerly a promising youngster with two performances already behind her, suddenly she was nothing more than the sister of Dannii Minogue, the star of what became one of the most successful television shows in Australia that year. Or at least that's how she was introduced. Not even her duet with Dannii on the show in 1986 performing The Eurythmics' hit 'Sisters Are Doing It For Themselves' could help.

'I don't want you to call me Dannii's sister,' she demanded at the time. 'Call me Kylie.'

As with most teenagers, Kylie's adolescent years were probably the most difficult and it was hardly surprising that Kylie was looking for something different.

That *something different* was, essentially, normal things like boys, alcohol and sex. Although no-one would ever be privy to any of that, either now or in the future. She made sure of that. Soon after she became famous, she decided to do away with all the diaries that she had kept up to that time. She literally burnt every one of them, simply to prevent prying eyes, journalists, reporters and the like from ever getting their hands on them. The one thing she didn't want to reveal to the world was anything of her private and personal life. And why should she?

After all, that would not have fitted in too well with the nice-girl-next-door image she wanted to project for her public persona. The kind of girl who, even at primary school was much more of a homely person.

She is probably now grateful that she did destroy her journals, considering the overall picture presented in other stories from that time. Some may have considered that her behaviour was outrageous, but others would disagree. She did no more than push at the boundaries just as most normal healthy young people do. A rebellious period is nothing more than a rite of passage that most teenagers pass through, and Kylie was no different.

'I was really shy! Well, I was sort of friends with everyone, so that was quite good. And even now I can adapt myself to what people want me to be. I'm more likely to be myself now, but I think that only comes with age and confidence, anyway. So yeah,

I was never picked in the sports team and never even a school play or anything like that.'

That normal girl had nonetheless been far more interested in acting than in anything related to school. Although an exceptional pianist as a child between the ages of seven and 13 – and she now regrets that she gave up playing – she wasn't, by her own admission, ever going to be academically inclined. Besides, what could a bunch of conforming school kids offer that rivalled the thrill of maybe some day being famous – being a star? Even if it was by accident as she adamantly insists today, 'I don't recall having aspirations as a young kid to really be famous, it more or less happened just by chance.'

A few weeks past her 16th birthday, however, through her determination to follow in Dannii's footsteps, to put herself on that road to stardom, she persevered and finally came up trumps sooner than she thought. And there was no way on earth she was going to let it pass her by.

Producer Alan Hardy was looking for young actors to fill nine parts in his latest project, a new children's serial called *The Henderson Kids*. Together with a thousand other aspiring youngsters, Kylie had responded to the newspaper advertisement summoning young hopefuls to attend.

Hardy did not recognise her when she turned up for the reading. Although she had met him on the set of *The Sullivans* some four years previously, the producer hardly noticed her at first among the hoards of others who had also turned up for the role that she was now desperately seeking.

Certainly, in the end, though, Hardy had no reservations about casting Kylie. As far as he was concerned, she would be absolutely the correct choice for the role of Charlotte Kernow, the tough-nosed urchin from a small working-class town who becomes the best friend of one of the principal characters played by Nadine Garner.

It was the story of the title characters Tamara Henderson (Garner) and her brother Steve, played by Paul Smith. After their mother is killed in a bizarre car accident, they go to live with their uncle, a policeman, coincidentally enough, who is stationed in a small city town, just outside Melbourne. With the land they inherit close to their uncle's home, the kids soon discover a cave situated on the property with ancient Aboriginal handprints. The rest of the story, and the series, focuses on how Steve, Tamara and friends fight to stop the cave getting into the hands of an unscrupulous developer.

Even with story, cast and crew firmly in place, there was still one thing left to finalise before shooting could commence on location in and around Melbourne. With Kylie being as blonde as Garner was, and to avoid having two blondes in the same show on screen at the same time, it was decided that, much to her disappointment, Kylie should be the one to dye her hair red.

Disappointed or not, on the set of *The Henderson Kids*, Kylie had no trouble exhibiting the determination that would later dictate her future career for those interested enough to read the signs. Less than two months into shooting the six-week series over six months, Kylie's quiet but determined ambition would take over, even if it did take her some time to discover it herself. By then, she had developed a tougher thread that eventually found its way on to the set. Even director Chris Langman noticed it.

It was no surprise then that as the series progressed so did her acting skills. She was only too aware that her ability was under the spotlight and maybe because of this awareness her tension, nervousness and any sense of insecurity eventually fell away, to the point that she was now getting into character at the studio door. Ideal, she thought, for getting in touch with the emotions she needed to access in front of the camera. And if all else failed, she could always rely on her keen sense of professionalism.

That natural talent also embraced her love of music which she would share throughout the production with Garner. In fact, one of the first things they did together to relax in between takes was to sing. 'It was during that time that I became more interested in singing,' remembers Kylie, 'just because me and another girl on the set, Nadine Garner, we always used to sing together. It's the first time I remember that I harmonised.'

Kylie's musical tastes as a child had occasionally followed listening to her parents' records such as The Beatles and the Rolling Stones, but her first love was disco music. In fact, the very first record she brought from her local record store had been a compilation album of early Seventies disco. She also adored the work of the Motown label, especially Marvin Gaye, The Four Tops and Stevie Wonder.

Abba and Madonna had also figured in her list of favourites at some time or another while growing up. And as for Prince, she was simply captivated. 'I'm a die-hard Prince fan,' she once raved. 'He's a really interesting person and the only artist I really admire as a fan. He's so outrageous and different. I used to scream at the film *Purple Rain*. I must have seen it countless times. His music is really innovative.'

While Kylie was already passionate about music, she could still be ambivalent about other areas of her life, such as religion. For Kylie, this remains an abstract concept at best, although regarding her personal beliefs she says, 'I'm not into formal religion, but I do believe there's some sort of God, though in what form I'm not sure.

'I think it's a little crazy that because of religions, which are supposed to symbolise peace, there are wars and conflicts between religions. I think that's nonsense. It's silly that people kill each other trying to prove that what they believe in is right and what the other believes isn't. What I believe is that there's something else, whatever it is you want it to be.

'It's a bit strange. Especially for me because I don't follow any rules. I wasn't brought up to go to church. I wasn't christened or baptised. I'm not educated in religion. I don't know what else to say about religion really. I think if you're happy with what you believe in, then great. Stick to it.'

With her work completed on *The Henderson Kids*, just two months after it aired in Australia on 11 May 1985, Kylie returned to school. In fact she had gone back following the wrap party, just missing the opening few weeks of her final year. With fond farewells and final harmonies performed with Garner, breaking up from the serial, however, proved to be far more difficult than anyone could imagine.

Realising how important it was that her education wouldn't suffer during filming, Kylie kept up with her studies with the help of on-set tutors. Even though she now had a run of acting work behind her, she had never forgotten her father's cautious counsel. Time and time again he would dutifully remind her to keep her feet firmly planted on the ground. He believed in the value of good education, and didn't want his daughter to find that she had nothing else to fall back on should she fail in her acting career.

'You combine school with work,' Kylie remembers. 'And I don't think I knew what I was doing anyway. It was just a lot of fun being on TV – excellent! I just did it. So when I left school I guess that was when I really took steps to be in entertainment and to get an agent. That's a hard enough step to take in the first place and I couldn't afford to get photos taken, so I had my brother take pictures of me.'

All the same, and in keeping with her dreams, she still hoped that one day she would have a successful acting career or perhaps something equally exciting in music. Certainly her time with Garner on the set of *The Henderson Kids*, singing to cast and crew, had made for fond memories and precious times, and with that in mind, she intended to do something about it.

'So the money I made from *The Henderson Kids*, which probably wasn't a lot, I put into making a demo of three songs, and I was having singing lessons.'

Despite half-hearted ideas for a secretarial training, a fashion course and, at one time, for a craft shop of her own, maybe she thought that acting was far better than drifting though her future for the sake of a career that she wouldn't have her heart in.

'I guess being a secretary wasn't my real aspiration,' Kylie later affirmed. 'I knew I wanted to do something in entertainment. I'd done acting through school, you know, I was doing a mini-series and things, but I just didn't have the confidence. I thought, you hear of more out of work actors than in work actors. And I figured I'd have to do something, so I guess I'll be a secretary or I'll do a business course or a fashion design course. I was really vague and I was just trying to pick something because they start forcing you in your final years of school.'

*The Henderson Kids* was not yet on air when the same production company, Crawford Productions, added their seal of approval to her performance by offering Kylie her next role. Although she would appear in just one episode, *The Zoo Family*, already a favourite on Australian television, probably offered Kylie her most challenging role yet.

Although not far off 17 at the time, the part she was now about to undertake catapulted her five years backwards to play Yvonne, an abused 12-year-old who is fostered into the family of a zoo caretaker during her summer vacation from school. From defacing zoo assets to releasing some of the kept animals out of their caged environment, she proves to be a nightmare, until she herself watches a frail kangaroo reunited with its mother. Only then does she decide to calm down her wild behaviour.

Kylie was probably exactly what Crawford Productions were looking for. It must have helped that she already looked like the character she was recruited to play, enhanced no doubt, by her younger-than-she-looked appearance. From that point of view, it's likely that both the makeup people and the wardrobe department had their load lightened considerably with her recruitment.

No sooner was her work on *The Zoo Family* complete than Kylie was starting work on yet another series. As if to prove just how good she actually was, when she attended the audition for *Fame and Misfortune,* a new six-part drama serial, she clearly beat fifty other girls to the part of Samantha, the devious, manipulative sister of the main central character.

The serial was produced and directed by Noel Price, and Kylie was also pleased to renew her friendship with her old ally from *The Henderson Kids,* Ben Mendelsohn, who had established himself as a highly promising newcomer.

On set, compared to the rest of the primarily juvenile cast, Kylie and Mendelsohn were considered old hands. Not that it mattered to 15-year-old cast member, Myles Collins. He proved an invaluable ally to Kylie both during and after filming. They would often spend time together, satisfying their mutual passion for music by secretly creeping into one of the neighbouring studios (mostly during weekends) on the same lot where they themselves were filming, to catch a glimpse of *Countdown* – Australia's favourite music show at that time. Coincidentally, two years later, Kylie's own success in music would result in her hosting that same programme, even if it was in the final year of its 13-year run.

Having completed work filming *Fame and Fortune* in May 1985, just as *The Henderson Kids* aired on national television, Kylie would suffer the first major setback of her acting career. Expecting to be recalled to reprise her role in *The Henderson Kids II*, producer Alan Hardy had the unenviable task of breaking the news to her that there was, quite simply, no role for her – Kylie's part in the new series had, surprisingly enough, been written out of the script.

Initially devastated, Kylie would not have long to mourn, however. After all, without this setback, she probably wouldn't have ended up as one of the most loved and cherished of all characters in Australian television history.

# THREE

# FIRST LOVE

Of the very few actors who have been in at the start of a television phenomenon and who continue to be associated with its success long after they have disappeared from the programme that established their names in the first place, none has wielded the kind of popularity that Kylie and Jason Donovan did in the late Eighties.

As Scott and Charlene, the boy and girl next door, the world's favourite teenage sweethearts, they were the golden couple that would take *Neighbours* from early evening comfort viewing to a top-rated Australian soap drama across three continents.

Kylie was 17 when she auditioned for the role of Charlene Mitchell, the headstrong, outspoken daughter of the equally stubborn and forthright Madge, in the then unremarkable nightly soap which had already been axed by one station. Even today, 16 years and dozens of cast changes later (since Madge died of breast cancer in 2001, only one character, Harold Bishop, Charlene's stepfather, remains from those early days) it still thrives – but without Kylie and Jason there was a good chance that it would not even have survived this long. Certainly not long enough to cross the globe.

Having clearly stood out from the crowd of the forty-plus other girls chasing the same role to make the indelible impression she did on casting director Jan Russ, Kylie began recording her first episode of *Neighbours* in February 1986.

Producer John Holmes agreed that Kylie Minogue would be the right choice for the role they were now looking to fill.

Although she was initially signed to appear for 13 weeks, following her debut on 18 April 1986, she was recruited for another 26, and in the end stayed on until June 1988. Exactly what the winning formula was for *Neighbours'* success is anyone's guess. Although over the years, the 20-minute, five-day-a-week programme has been picked over, discussed, dissected and dismissed, one cannot argue the fact that it caught the imagination of youngsters, teens and mum and dads.

The idea of making *Neighbours* was the brainchild of Reg Watson, the veteran executive producer at Grundy Television. At that time, established and confident, he was best known for masterminding other such Australian hits as *Sons and Daughters* and *The Young Doctors*, both of which would subsequently cross the ocean to acquire dedicated followings in other territories across the globe. And although *Neighbours* would eventually win through in the ratings war, it was initially purchased for British viewing as a cheap buy.

Another series that was bought for UK television was *Prisoner,* which would go on to become one the biggest cult soap dramas of the Eighties, and still is to this day in some territories whenever it has a rerun. Of course by the time it reached British screens, it had undergone a change of title to *Prisoner Cell Block H* to avoid confusion and possibly infringement problems with Patrick McGoohan's cult classic series *The Prisoner*.

Watson, however, was no stranger to British television production. He had already notched up an impressive résumé of other shows, in Britain, for almost a decade. One of the most successful that he worked on was *Crossroads* (just recently resurrected opposite the early evening slot for *Neighbours*).

Overall though, the one thing that could be said about a British soap opera was that it never really contained much more than the mundane when compared to the high drama, excitement and scandal at the heart of those being produced in America at that time.

From that point of view, perhaps Watson considered that the Australian market was missing something. Certainly, there had never been anything based around ordinary folk in an ordinary neighbourhood, fighting ordinary battles against the slings and arrows of mildly outrageous life. If the original intention was for *Neighbours* to fill that gap, to reflect that gentle community spirit, then it worked.

Although there were plenty of other shows addressing bigger issues and offering more colourful drama, in the fictional Erinsborough, there would be no arch-villains, no shock-horror, no twisted plots and no whodunit ending. Neither would there be any sex, bare breasts, dope, guns or violence. First and foremost, *Neighbours* would be a drama about friendship.

In the end, though, the theory fell short of the promise. When the programme first aired on Channel Seven in Australia on 18 March 1985, in the 5.30pm slot before the early evening news, viewers already conditioned to expect the dramatic were disappointed. If Watson had the belief that such conventions are there to be broken and that an audience will happily watch you break them as long as they are entertained, then on this occasion, it hadn't worked. In fact, so poor were the ratings, except for around Melbourne, that by November, it was quickly dropped from the schedules. Just eight months after it had launched.

And then out of the blue, when all was thought to be lost, the rival Channel Ten network announced that they would be re-launching the programme within the next two months. Whatever the reason for the takeover, *Neighbours'* new home was well aware of its potential and had decided to give it another try with just a few subtle adjustments – there would be no drastic changes to the original concept.

*Neighbours* was originally conceived and designed to exert a universal appeal with characters from every walk of life repre-sented in each of the episodes – every age group from child to grandparent, a variety of socio-economic groups from jobbing gardener through artisan, to established professional and self-made wealthy entrepreneurs. There would be someone for every viewer to relate to and connect with.

From an analysis of the viewing figures made during its first run on Channel Seven, the strongest fan base for the programme was, by far, the 14- to 18-year-olds. And Channel Ten planned to ensure that it was that age group in particular that would continue to be targeted with characters and storylines with which they could identify and engage.

Now the programme would focus on the kind of representa-tive young individuals who would enjoy the same lifestyle, experi-ences, struggles and dramas as the audience the show was setting out to capture in its re-launch.

Nowhere was that more evident than with the introduc-tion of a new, recast Scott Robinson. Now played by Jason

Donovan, he was one of the main characters who proved far more popular with the new targeted audience than the predecessor had. And if he was going to have a girlfriend, then who better than Kylie?

Certainly that was the opinion of the studio heads at Channel Ten. But if *Neighbours* was going to succeed, come what may, so would the commitment to promote the show. That's why the station was prepared to invest in a huge publicity trail that would ensure their instincts could not be proven wrong.

The majority of the cast and crew must have the found the new schedules arduous. In addition to the 12-hour working days that were now instituted (every episode had 25 one-minute scenes, each taking half-an-hour to rehearse and tape) and evenings usually spent going over the lines for the next day, there were also the long drives and helicopter rides across the country for radio and press interviews and personal appearances at clubs and shopping centres.

They accepted the fact that publicity and promotion was part and parcel of the deal of being on *Neighbours*. Or at least that's what they were told by Brian Walsh, then head of promotion and publicity in charge of the marketing campaigns that were now being devised. Besides, the show had already been axed once before and if that happened again, everyone was well aware that they would all be out of work.

In fact, out of everyone, it was Kylie and Jason who embraced the idea with the most enthusiasm. Although Kylie had a great attitude, at the time, towards making it work, she had no idea how poorly the show had previously been received. She believed, perhaps naively, that it was the best thing that had ever happened – and for her career it certainly was.

With the *Neighbours* re-launch firmly set for 20 January 1986, expectations were running high. Even though the initial weeks proved difficult, with ratings barely changed, the cast must have been wondering whether all their efforts, with endless round of personal appearances to boost the show's appeal, had been worthwhile.

But perhaps none of that was needed. Once Jason and Kylie came into the picture things began to improve immensely – as far as ratings were concerned, at least. Formerly nothing more than a couple of promising youngsters, before they knew what was happening Kylie and Jason were in the show and were suddenly the stars of what became one of the most popular television soaps in Australia that year. With Jason and Kylie, the viewing figures began to soar. They put *Neighbours* firmly on the map and won the hearts of a generation.

Although there were others among the ensemble cast, such as Guy Pearce, Elaine Smith, Peter O'Brien and later Craig McLachlan, who were all crucial to the show, it seemed that everyone, the press in particular, simply adored Kylie and Jason as much as their alter egos, Charlene and Scott.

'I remember a few cast members were in the green room at Channel 10 and someone came in and said that *Neighbours* was being played in England,' Kylie recalls. 'We thought a few people would see it: a couple of kids home sick from school and maybe a bored mum. Then we started hearing reports that doctors' surgeries were changing their hours and kids were leaving school early to see the show. There was such a buzz.'

And when that happened, Brian Walsh must have heaved an enormous sigh of relief. After all the effort, it seemed that his previously untried publicity drives had actually paid dividends for real. No matter how basic the scripts may have been, or how inadequate the sets, like Kylie and Jason, his belief in the show had shone through time and again. The same belief that would eventually spread across Australia.

In little more than nine weeks since its re-launch *Neighbours'* viewing figures had reached epidemic proportions and, with the endless press coverage indicating as much, it seemed that the show was a success at last. Certainly by the end of 1986, it was only the Sydney newspapers that weren't covering the soap, despite the crowds that gathered for promotional events at shopping malls around the city each weekend. Curiously, the Sydney press expressed no interest whatsoever, even though it was going on right under their noses – not even when the crowds rapidly grew into thousands.

In fact it took direct persuasion to convince them otherwise. With a film crew on hand, Brian Walsh shot footage of the crowds attending each of the events, and then with a note of explanation as to why thousands of fans were rioting everywhere they went, he sent the note and tapes out to every newspaper and magazine in Australia.

This was a devastatingly effective tactic.

*Neighbours'* stock was rising ever higher, partly through Walsh's genius for generating hype but also because the storylines were getting better and better and were essential viewing, particularly if you were a teenager.

And nowhere was that better expressed than in a storyline which was dead on course for Charlene and Scott's first screen kiss on an isolated beach. And what better than to invite the *Daily Mirror* to witness the moment? Which of course, they did, with a front-page headline that read:

TV SHOCK: TEEN SEX ON TV TONIGHT.

But of course, viewers expecting a raunchy episode were simply disappointed. It really was only a kiss. All the same the Sydney newspapers made a meal out of it, and for the time being at least *Neighbours* was front-page news. From that point onward, of course, the power of celebrity kicked in. Kylie and Jason were the nation's favourite stars and their faces suddenly took up residence on most of the teen magazines, even on the cover of *TV Week*, Australia's leading listing magazine.

Still there were those among the more established names on the show who seemed less than enthusiastic about this new turn of events. Having seen themselves as the real actors, as the whole bedrock of the show, they weren't about to relinquish their standing. As far as they were concerned, the younger element of the cast, they thought, were nothing more than amateurs simply recruited to boost the popularity of the programme for their good looks and inept talent. What they seemed to forget, however, was that without the huge promotional input and efforts from Kylie and Jason and others like Guy Pearce and Peter O'Brien, the show wouldn't have been the success it was, and with no show, they too would have been looking for new work.

Whatever the experienced actors thought of her talent, the one accusation nobody could ever level at Kylie was a lack of professionalism. She never missed a call. She was always on time for work. And whenever she was on set, her mind was focused fully on the task ahead.

Exactly what made Charlene such compulsive viewing is still a mystery. Kylie couldn't understand it either – she was as mystified as anyone. Maybe, Kylie shrugs, it's because she is 'an average teenager who has problems with her boyfriend and with getting a career started. She's a bit of a rebel, and they probably relate to that.'

It was much the same story when *Neighbours* first appeared on British television at midday on 26 October 1986. Even though Charlene and Scott wouldn't appear for at least another eight months, it was still a runaway success. By which time, of course, Kylie and Jason were now lovers off screen as well as on.

Certainly she didn't find it difficult to avoid the people she knew were out to puncture her balloon. When she wasn't in front of the camera, she spent most of her time hanging out with Jason, adding fuel to the already inflamed speculation about an off-screen relationship.

Both cast and crew were well aware from the start that Kylie and Jason were with each other almost every minute of the day. If not working on screen together, they were stealing secret moments with each other as soon as they stepped off the set.

Their attraction, some say, was an instant connection. Well, it was once Kylie had reminded Jason who she was. She, of course, had recognised him immediately, from their time together, albeit briefly, on the set of *Skyways*, when the plump 12-year-old Jason had played tiny blonde Kylie's brother. But when she bounced up to him that first day on the *Neighbours* set, much to her chagrin, her enthusiastic greeting drew a blank.

Physically she had changed a great deal less than he had. The chunky, floppy-haired kid had now filled out to exhibit all the charms that would cause a vast number of schoolgirls on both sides of the Equator to fall for him in an instant, especially Kylie. The little blonde girl, however, had grown into a desirable young woman. And fortunately, he made the connection to their past just in time to stop Kylie bursting into tears.

Although both were now actors, they didn't really share the same childhood backgrounds. Kylie had grown up in what could best be described as a conventional environment, raised by middle-class working parents, while Jason hailed from a theatrical family and upbringing.

As long as he could remember, he had always been a resilient child – he had to be – and like Kylie, had grown up overshadowed by family fame. As the only child of a former high-profile model and one of Australia's best-known television actors, his birth on 1 June 1968 in Malvern, Melbourne was headline news.

Of course, at times he wished his parents were still together. His mother, Sue McIntosh, had left the family to end up as a television newsreader when Jason was just five years old. And that, he confessed later, would be the only time he saw her – on a television screen reading the nightly news.

His father was Terence Donovan, an already well-known face on several of Australia's best-loved television police dramas who would even land himself a small role in *Neighbours* for a few years, long after Jason and Kylie had left the show. On top of looking after an acting career, of course, he had also raised Jason on his own until he later remarried.

By then, of course their relationship – as with most lone parents – was solid as a rock. Not only that but in those eight years, he had raised Jason with the same respect he would an equal. Now in turn Terry was Jason's best friend and soul mate. The one person that Jason would turn to for advice and counsel.

Still, by the time Jason joined *Neighbours*, he already had a string of Australian television roles behind him in such dramas as *I Can Jump Puddles*, *Golden and Pennies*, *Home*, *Marshal*, and *Skyways* of course. And he was still living with his father – well, sort of. It was a bungalow at the back of Terry's house in

Melbourne. But to Jason, and now Kylie, it was home. It was their safe haven away from prying eyes.

Jason, of course, was in the same position as Kylie was. He had experienced the culture shock of stepping off a school bus into a limousine, and in the course of just a few months, just as she had, was thrown headfirst into the glare of the media spotlight. A new and potentially scary experience for each of them.

He also understood the stresses and pressures of their punishing work schedule better than anyone in Kylie's nine-to-five family possibly could. The rehearsal, recording and promotion were gruelling enough without having to worry about the 16-hour days and no free time on weekends. It was hardly surprising they spent the precious little leisure they had together.

They were also as straight as they could be about their relationship. Or at least they were around the set. As far as the other cast members on *Neighbours* were concerned, it was an open secret. Never once did they attempt to hide the fact. Every off-camera minute, it seemed, they used as an excuse to spend time with each other even if only for a few seconds.

Their relationship on screen, however, was far more dramatic than it was off screen. Problems and friction were the keywords to turn their romance into a complicated series of ups-and-downs and offs-and-ons. The scriptwriters were only too aware of that. And they made sure that Scott and Charlene had plenty of both at every possible moment.

Charlene's rapport with her mother Madge, for instance, would be strewn with hurdles. And when she moved in with the Robinson family, more disasters occurred with the couple tripping over Scott's little sister Lucy and traumas with the strait-laced attitude of Scott's dad Jim. Although today much of this probably sounds rather lame, at the time it was guaranteed to keep *Neighbours* in the ratings.

There were, of course, the inevitable round of teenage quandaries about sex, self-image, insecurity and identity. How would Scott respond when he found out his girl wasn't a virgin? Why shouldn't a girl, Charlene in this case, be a motor mechanic? And what was so great about obtaining good school grades, among other teen turmoil and upsets?

For one scene, the script called for Charlene to lose her cool completely and throw a punch at Scott. Soon after the filming of that scene had been completed, Kylie had found herself answering to the nickname of 'Bruiser' for weeks on end after the blow she made connected a little too realistically and she had actually laid Jason out on the studio floor for real, much the same as Cher had done when she actually slapped Winona Ryder across the face during the shooting of the penultimate scene in the 1990 movie *Mermaids*. But wasn't that the point of acting, to make the unbelievable believable? Kylie, it seemed, could do that as well.

In contrast to their degenerating relationship on screen, the real-life couple had a much more genuine bond of friendship and love, of course, than those they were playing out for the camera. Or at least they thought they did. Right up to the time when studio bosses realised what was actually going on – that their two stars were in a real-life relationship. But Brian Walsh was only marginally concerned.

Walsh had a talent for turning anything, good or bad, into a story that could hook media attention, especially the press. Whether he was right in his belief that news of a real-life romance between his star couple would damage both their popularity and the show's rating, he didn't really know. But what he did know was the opportunity to set up an ambiguous situation would set curiosity buzzing and the public guessing. At least it would provide the tabloids with some new morsels of gossip.

Kylie and Jason were instructed to be circumspect, give guarded, noncommittal answers to media questions about their relationship, and avoid giveaway displays of affection on the rare occasions their heavy workload allowed them to enjoy a night out together, whether at a restaurant, nightclub or cinema. It was made crystal clear from this point onwards that they must make loyalty to the show their first priority, and if that meant keeping their personal feelings under wraps, then so be it.

Whatever the motivation for Walsh, the ruling set a new tone for the public perception of the on–off and on again Kylie and Jason romance which, in the eyes of the outside world, would last as long as the media and public wanted to believe it. It also kept the journalists on their toes. Were they … weren't they? It would always give the tabloids something to speculate about.

At the end of 1986 the couple were rewarded with a holiday in Bali for having gone along with the studio rules and wishes. They took off for the beautiful Polynesian island for a couple of weeks' rest and recreation away from the public gaze. Not to miss out, Walsh, familiar with dealing with such Hollywood-style secrets, also went along. Probably to make sure their frolicking was kept away from prying eyes.

For Kylie and Jason, the vacation would provide a welcome respite from the daily harassment of the popular press – and from the onslaught that was about to happen on their return.

By the beginning of January 1987, Kylie and Jason had the world at their feet. The runaway success of *Neighbours* on both Australian and British television firmly established the couple among the upper echelon of small screen celebrities. This was evident from the first time they appeared together on the front of *TV Week*, the premier national listings magazine, and the dozens of other cover shots that followed.

Not a day passed when the *Neighbours* press office didn't receive a request for interviews, photos and the like. Although their rise to stardom would seem to defy logic, they nevertheless continued to strike an affectionate chord with audiences, fans and the media. Neither would it be long before devotees began to feel that they were as familiar with Kylie and Jason as with their on-screen counterparts Charlene and Scott.

Speaking of their aspirations and future plans both in and (more importantly) out of the celebrity spotlight probably helped. It allowed audiences to get to know them as ordinary people and not as stars. Kylie herself spoke about the arts and crafts interest she had maintained since she was a child, and the ideas she still kept for opening a coffee or gift shop in her hometown some time in the future.

Like most intelligent celebrities, she was only too aware that her new-found fame and fortune could end as quickly as it had taken off. And if that happened, she was determined to have a safety net already in place. It was what her father had insisted upon: that she should have something to fall back on.

Jason's professed dream for the future was to prove more accurate than the one Kylie had in mind at the time. Revealing an ambition that his father would have identified with completely, he said that he would one day like to have the opportunity to work live on stage in the sort of musicals that have long captured the spirit of London's theatreland and New York's Broadway. In fact, Jason's own lead role in the West End production of *Joseph and the Amazing Technicolor Dreamcoat* did, in early 1992, win him the acclaim he had so long yearned for.

But when asked what she intended to buy with the considerable wealth *Neighbours* was amassing for her, Kylie was quick to reply. She expressed a desire for a horse, but at the same time had to admit that her hectic schedule would not allow her such pleasurable pastimes. In response to the same question, Jason, in his usual straightforward manner, said that he would save every penny towards his first house.

Most intriguing of all was the question that they were inevitably asked in every interview – whether they were romantically involved with each other off-screen as well as on. But every time that was put to them, they would just keep to the story Brian Walsh had told them to tell. They were simply good friends. Even though there was much speculation of a real-life relationship, none of that, they insisted, was true.

By now, of course, Kylie and Jason fan hysteria was taking hold. This had been evident from when they finally made the front pages of the Sydney newspapers late in 1986, thanks to Walsh's efforts and much to his satisfaction. Now Kylie and Jason could capitalise on their true media triumph with high-profile personal appearances in the city.

One of those occasions was at Sydney's prestigious Royal Easter Show at the end of March 1987. With echoes of the fan hysteria that greeted The Beatles' first American tour in the early Sixties, thousands of screaming teenagers fought their way to catch a glimpse of the couple. Kylie 'n' Jasonmania, it seemed, had well and truly arrived.

With more than four dozen extra police officers recruited to rescue them from the crush of the boisterous crowds, now out of control, the recruits had no other choice but to shove the couple unceremoniously into the back of one of their vans to get them

back to safety. But even that took over forty minutes. More
worrying was the toll of those injured in the crush. One was taken
to hospital; four others needed treatment after receiving minor
but still significant injuries.

Not all their appearances were greeted with such madness.
By the time they received the final, gold-plated evidence of their
success in April 1987, Kylie and Jason were the biggest craze in
Australian television history. The ultimate accolade, the icing on
the cake, to this success came exactly a year after Kylie had first
appeared on *Neighbours*. It was at the annual live-to-air *TV Week*
Logie Awards – the Australian equivalent to Britain's National
Television Awards and the BAFTAs. Even though Jason just
narrowly pipped Kylie for the Best New Talent award, the
evening was Kylie's when she walked away with the Most Popular
Actress nomination. She was the youngest person ever to do so
and still is to this day.

The ceremony and media coverage that both Kylie and Jason
had garnered from the awards night were further proof, if any
were needed, of their undeniable appeal. And with knowledge of
how much attention that could hold, they decided, in the
momentum of success, to announce their involvement with a
new government anti-drugs campaign aimed at teenagers.

In fact, if rumours are to be believed, then it would be almost
ironic that years later, Jason was allegedly said to have been a regular marijuana smoker himself during this time. Equally ironically,
of course, was when he collapsed outside Johnny Depp's Viper
Room in Los Angeles – in January 1995 – almost echoing the River
Phoenix tragedy at the club just fifteen months earlier. Yet he
considered it a great deal less risky than those addicted to alcohol.

Although today his drugs versus alcohol standpoint may be
shared by others, objection to drug use in the late Eighties couldn't

have been higher. In contrast, of course, Kylie's campaigning came straight from the heart. She hardly ever touched alcohol, aside from the odd glass of wine here and there, and dope was anathema to her. Her view was simple. It was decadent, despicable and damaging.

With reported fallouts between the couple, it appeared that Kylie was less than pleased by Jason's attitude towards drugs. Maybe she had hoped that their involvement in the government campaign would have convinced Jason to think twice about his alleged habit. If any of that was true, then Kylie would be faced with having to hide the truth at all costs. What seemed to escape Jason's attention was the fact that such public revelations could have put both their future careers and ethics very much under question.

Her concern about such matters was also mirrored on the set, not only by drugs issues which were resolutely avoided, but by a policy decision not to introduce topics which might offend and upset young fans – or perhaps their parents. Wasn't it they who should exercise a modicum of control over their offsprings' viewing habits?

*Neighbours* at that time was purely wholesome and the producers went to considerable lengths to maintain that criteria. Any storyline considered to overstep the boundaries of decency was firmly expunged. On one occasion, though not without some discussion, an entire half day of recording was written off simply because the prospect of Charlene having a discussion with her mother about going on the Pill was regarded as inappropriate and unacceptable for primetime teenage audiences.

Much later, of course, it emerged that the goings-on behind the scenes were not without drama. Neither, apparently, was life on the set as squeaky-clean and fresh-faced as many had been led to believe. When the show had taken off in Britain so successfully, some of Kylie and Jason's colleagues from *Neighbours* had crossed the world to pursue the new career opportunities that their sudden success had opened up for them. It was then that they would talk openly to the British popular press. And the stories they were telling did not always tally with the official ones put out by the studio.

One of those was Guy Pearce, a contemporary of Kylie and Jason in the early days, who later starred in such movies as *The Adventures of Priscilla, Queen of the Desert, LA Confidential* and *Memento*. Guy always sang her praises, and would be the first to applaud her sense of fun. As far as he was concerned, she was the mastermind behind all the practical jokes on set, such as the coffee bar cream bun fights, the strategically placed water balloons and birthday strippergrams. But he also told stories of how Kylie and co-star Annie Jones frequently swam and horsed around topless at pool parties, and no one even batted an eyelid.

'Kylie has a great body and she enjoyed showing it off. We'd all charge down to the pool, whip our clothes off and jump in. Kylie and Annie didn't give a damn about going topless – we were great mates and there was nothing sexual in it. Kylie would joke that if the press could see us they'd have a field day.'

But according to Pearce, it was Kylie's bad language that made him laugh the most. 'She may seem squeaky-clean, but she had a tongue on her like a Sydney trucker. We all knew each other well so we all swore like troopers. But I remember Kylie in partic-ular because when she let rip – she really let rip. One of Kylie's tricks was to deliberately swear if she thought a scene was going poorly to make sure it got re-shot.'

Whether she did or didn't and whatever went on between scenes, it didn't really matter. There was still a large element of self-imposed censorship worked into the scripts: although it would be true to say that it was very much a guarded approach, it would still lead to shock horror among audiences when news leaked out that Scott and Charlene were proposing to move in together. More than that, it simply fuelled outrage among the more conservative fans who regarded Ramsay Street as the final bastion of a world of innocence, decency and high principles.

Even though the public's reaction was reflected right there among the more strait-laced residents of the street, surely such a storyline would simply be abandoned at the eleventh hour. But it wasn't. The idea was to portray Scott and Charlene as young and very much in love with their passion for each other obviously running high, just as in real life. With critical objections voiced before filming even began, and growing insistently louder as the episode screening drew closer, the only solution, it was decided, was to get them safely married, and as quickly as possible.

The union of Charlene Mitchell and Scott Robinson was the wedding of the decade. By the time the big day arrived, in early July 1987, it had already been hyped to such an extent that no one in Australia could possibly have been unaware that it was happening.

Even *Time* magazine fell under the spell, and was prepared to compromise its reputation as a serious publication. The cover of an early July issue of the Australian edition carried a heart-shaped picture of the happy couple, and the issue itself was dedicated to 'all those who are in love and all those who can remember'.

On the morning before the episode was aired, Kylie and Jason took part in yet another of the publicity stunts arranged by Brian Walsh. This time he had arranged a wedding breakfast staged at a suburban shopping centre in Sydney. From one point of view, it was a huge success. It had attracted over 4,000 frantic young fans. But for some, the excitement of the occasion proved too much. Once again, the event had the crowd out of control and the police rushing in to chaperone a flustered Kylie and Jason away to safety under their guarded protection. Not for the first time, fans were injured and needed to be taken to hospital for treatment. Kylie, of course, found the whole experience quite frightening, and it wouldn't be too long before she would call a halt to the madness.

It may have been the biggest day of the year for fans, but for Kylie and Jason, Charlene and Scott's wedding was just another episode to record: an episode which would attract the highest ever ratings for a soap opera on Australian television, but all in a day's work nonetheless.

However, when it came time for Jason to kiss the bride, insisted one crew member, it was impossible to believe that they were just friends. From that moment onwards, it seemed that Walsh's carefully maintained no-romance ruling was all but doomed. He felt things were now getting out of control and that it wouldn't be long before the 'just good friends' façade was completely blown.

The year had already been eventful, as much for Jason and Kylie as it had been for Scott and Charlene. Kylie, increasingly restless, wanted a new challenge. Her love of music had never waned, not since she had made her guest appearance with sister Dannii on *Young Talent Time*, back in 1986.

Not only that, but she had also taken part in a benefit concert for her Australian Rules football team at the request of Alan Hardy, also a supporter, and the producer who had, to all intents and purposes, given Kylie her first opportunities as an actress. It was here that she performed a duet of Sonny and Cher's 1965 hit 'I Got You Babe' with local actor Jon Waters, and another backed by several members of the *Neighbours* house band, as they were then known. As expected, or perhaps not, the performance went down a storm with the crowd who demanded an encore.

Without any other songs prepared, Kylie and the *Neighbours* band decided upon 'The Locomotion', Little Eva's Sixties dance classic which they had regularly performed in their after-work jamming sessions. It had been the first song Kylie had performed in front of her co-stars when she was initially pestered to join the band. And one that would leave her colleagues in no doubt of the remarkable vocal talent she had kept locked up in her closet. Those impromptu sessions would now prove invaluable when she returned out on to the stage that night to perform the song that would alter the course of her career – and her life – forever.

Alan Dale, who played Kylie's father-in-law Jim Robinson, and who was also a member of the house band, remembers that night very well because 'Locomotion' was one of the songs they had worked out to play, 'so when she arrived, we asked her if she could sing it, and as it happened she knew the words and sang it.

'She was standing about three feet in front of me, right in front of me, and we sort of moved into it, you know, "C'mon baby, do the locomotion," and off she went. When she'd finished, silence fell, we looked at each other, couldn't believe it. Here was this tiny little girl who looked great, and was great, who could sing like an angel as well. Really, *really* well. She was a *good* singer.'

Before anybody knew what was happening, Kylie had that very same song at Number One in the Australian record charts, in July 1987, more or less two weeks after the *Neighbours* wedding episode had been aired. It must have been beyond her wildest dreams at that time or in fact anybody else's, but Kylie's

'Locomotion' became the biggest selling single of the 1980s in Australia, and the biggest selling single in the history of Mushroom Records – and still is to this day.

The success of the surprise hit record caused even more chaos to her life than she thought possible. She was now only too aware that, like many others before her, she would require a personal manager to handle things on her behalf.

# FOUR

# SOAP STAR
# TO POP IDOL

Discovering Kylie's musical talent has become the claim to fame of so many different parties that the solid truth may never be known. It is often maintained that it was all her own idea and that a copy of the tape she had recorded was then given to Mushroom Records by one of her friends.

Another theory is that Mushroom's managing director Gary Ashley, and British PWL engineer Mike Duffy, working on secondment to Mushroom, were both at the football benefit at which Kylie performed alongside her *Neighbours* co-stars, and after watching her performance that night quickly set up a recording session for her. It is why both have individually been named through the years as the talent spotters who first spotted her.

The third and final version of events is probably the correct one and, to some, the most believable account of how it happened. In many quarters it is thought to have been Greg Petherick who was responsible for getting the whole thing up and running. He was an in-house producer at Channel Ten, working on an Australian music show in a studio adjacent to the *Neighbours* set, and had known the Minogue family for a few years by the time Kylie had joined the channel.

From his work in television, he also knew sound engineer Kaj Dahlstrom who ran Sing Sing recording studios and at that time didn't have much other work on. Petherick apparently encouraged him to take on the task and risk, at his own expense, recording, producing and picking up the tab for the demo tape, and if things went according to plan, and they got a record deal, he would, of course, be paid for his trouble.

Although Kylie had recorded a demo with her fee from *The Henderson Kids*, it was not the same session that produced her demo of 'Locomotion'. In fact, out of the three tracks she had laid down at a recording studio in Melbourne 18 months earlier, 'Locomotion' certainly wasn't among them.

'All I can remember is crying because I was so nervous,' Kylie recalls. But it also proves that her discovery wasn't quite out of the blue as it once appeared, even if by her own reckoning, she never intended to be a singer.

'I remember doing a demo tape when I was 17, three songs, the wereabouts of which are unknown at this point, so someone has got a demo of me where I sound like Mickey Mouse singing 'Dim All the Lights' by Donna Summer, 'New Attitude' by Patti LaBelle and 'Just Once' by Quincy Jones. I sure picked them, didn't I?'.

If anything, the thought of a 17-year-old in a recording studio in 1985 suggests that she must have harboured some ambition to be discovered and catapulted into instant pop stardom, even if she was simply trying to increase her appeal to casting directors.

'The more things you can do the better,' she explains. 'Can

you paraglide? Me? Sure. Rollerskate? No problem. Sing? Here's my tape.'

Whichever is the correct version and whatever the origins of the 'Locomotion' demo tape, as soon as it was in the hands of Amanda Pelham, Mushroom's promotions manager, things certainly began to take shape. Indeed, it was Pelham's keenly honed marketing instincts that immediately zeroed in on the enormous possibilities that were now evident.

In Australia, and elsewhere, Kylie was *the* face. She had all but taken up permanent residence on the covers of most of the teen magazines and most of the other popular press at that time, so it was obvious that the potential for crossover promotion was immense. Wasn't that how to sell records? Pelham thought so, and quickly came up with the idea of aiming the record at exactly the same targeted audience as Channel Ten had for *Neighbours*. Namely all the young adolescent girls for whom Kylie was now both an idol and a role model.

According to legend, the first meeting Kylie had in the boardroom of the Mushroom offices was with Pelham, Gary Ashley and Kylie's dad, Ron Minogue, who from the start had firmly installed himself as his daughter's manager and financial advisor.

While Kylie sat quietly in a corner, perhaps slightly overawed by the surroundings of the gold and platinum disc awards that lined the walls, her father would negotiate the best deal he knew how. Although a reputable local accountant for many years, with a keen eye for most money matters, this was something quite alien to him. This was the music business. Something he knew very little about, as he himself would probably have admitted. But present now as both Kylie's father, acting on behalf of his young and naive daughter, as well as her newly appointed business manager, he fought for the best deal possible, and to clarify all details of any contract that Kylie may be offered.

It was only when a decision was later made and contracts signed that Mushroom – then Australia's premier independent record label – or rather Pelham, set about re-producing Kylie's demo with the aim of releasing a single to coincide with the wedding of Scott and Charlene.

For the task of rebuilding the music track but retaining the original vocals, they recruited Mike Duffy – one of those who have been credited as having discovered Kylie – to oversee the project. At that time he was working for a leading Melbourne studio on a three-month secondment from PWL, the London-based production company run by producer Pete Waterman.

Waterman was one-third of the legendary partnership of hitmakers Stock, Aitken and Waterman to whom top names such as Rick Astley and Bananarama already owed their success. Their exhilarating, upbeat dance sound was distinctive, infectious and highly marketable – but at that stage Kylie could have had no idea of the impact that the connection with Waterman would make on the rest of her life.

Just two weeks after the *Neighbours* wedding of the year, Mushroom released 'Locomotion' – Kylie's version of the pop classic written by hitmakers Carole King and Gerry Goffin. The song that had already been a wordwide hit for Little Eva back in 1962.

For Kylie, hearing herself on local radio for the first time was like one of those defining moments we all experience. She was in the comfort of her own home with her family, when she was tuned in, listening, ready and waiting. She truly had no idea that the record would figure in the charts at all, let alone in the Top

Ten. When the DJ finally announced that she was at Number One, she could hardly believe it.

But she was. And a few days after that, 'Locomotion' was also Number One in the national charts, where it remained for the next two months and went on to become the best-selling single of the decade in Australia. And by November 1987, it had also reached Number One in Hong Kong and New Zealand.

It was during the success of 'Locomotion' that something happened that would alter the course of Kylie's life forever. Recalling the time when she was working on *Fame and Misfortune* two years earlier, when she would sneak into the nearby *Countdown* studio to watch the glitzy, high-profile pop music programme being recorded, she was now – as the series approached its final show – invited to the final *Countdown* Music Awards in Sydney. But at the time, of course, she had no idea of how significant the occasion would be. It was the first time she met INXS vocalist, Michael Hutchence.

If anything, Kylie was completely taken by surprise. Even star-struck perhaps. Although she had thoroughly enjoyed the awards ceremony, 'I was worried that a lot of the famous big-time rock music people would look down on me as just a soapie star moving in on their area and zooming up the chart. But they were all really nice. Michael Hutchence made an effort to come over and say hi, which was good of him.'

It was also becoming clear that from now on such events would form a significant part of Kylie's life. The one sure thing about having a hit record is that it will always generate an almost endless list of requests for personal appearances. And a hit record by an attractive young woman who is already a huge favourite with the television community can only result in a lifestyle that needs serious organisation and planning.

The success of 'Locomotion' and the impact it was already having on Kylie's hectic round of filming schedules and personal appearance commitments would, she thought, be best handled by an experienced manager. And although Ron Minogue had done a remarkable job of looking after both his daughters in their professional lives, he probably realised, now more than ever, that the sudden bedlam of attention Kylie was receiving from the media was way outside his experience.

Even though Amanda Pelham at Mushroom Records had handled everything up to this point she wasn't in a position to manage Kylie or even organise her now rapidly escalating diary. That would have left her little time for her other duties at the record label. In the end, it was left to Mushroom executives to look around for a likely candidate to take on their new signing.

Gary Ashley's first choice of manager was Terry Blamey, a 36-year-old talent booker for the cabaret circuit, who ran his own booking agency Pace Entertainment out of the record company's Melbourne offices.

Blamey may have lacked experience in managing pop singers at that time, but he did manage one other of sorts, and did have one chart success under his belt.

Nonetheless, according to Ashley, Blamey was very down to earth, and a family man who would find it easy to deal with the Minogue family on a professional and personal level. He was straight down the line, would say what he thought of something, and would let Kylie have a say in everything she did, should she want that.

Although he was intrigued about 'this new kid, Kylie', Blamey was reported to have been initially reluctant to take her on. Even after he agreed to do it, it was probably not until he met up with Kylie and her parents that he realised her potential.

From that moment with Mushroom's and the Minogues' endorsement, Blamey became Kylie's personal manager, and still is to this day, 14 years later, which in itself is unusual.

Unusual that is when you consider how the record industry is notoriously famous for artists changing and swapping management and representatives as regular as clockwork. That alone is a testament to their belief in each other. 'Yeah,' jokes Kylie. 'Mainly it's because we tell equally bad jokes! We've been on a lot of flights together.'

From this point onwards, Kylie's life would be quite different from the one she had come to know. With Blamey and Mushroom in control of her career, much of her free time would be spent in an endless round of media engagements. Not surprising really when you consider that she had gone from being an award-winning actress in a top-rated television soap to fielding jibes from cast and crew members about her ambitions to be a singer and then still being at the top of the chart by the end of August 1987 with 'Locomotion'.

The usual leisurely weekend breakfasts with Jason at their bungalow hideaway were now a thing of the past. When she wasn't promoting *Neighbours* she was ensuring that she was getting the correct exposure to keep her record in the charts as long as possible. This wasn't entirely uncharted territory to her of course. She had already experienced the same kind of pressure during the early days of *Neighbours*.

Although it does not appear to have affected her work or her performances, it was around this time that Kylie began to succumb to the pressure, with one minor ailment after another. Although, the underlying stress that was the cause of this physical exhaustion was quite understandable, Kylie had a great deal of pride in her professional approach to work – something she would later term her 'hideous professionalism' – she kept it hidden to all but her closest family and friends. She had to strike while the iron was hot, and there were new plans afoot.

By November 1987, 'Locomotion' was still at Number One in Hong Kong and New Zealand, but the one thing Kylie had not yet been able to do was establish herself in Britain, either as a singer or actress. With two weeks off from *Neighbours* she boarded a plane for London. Pete Waterman, she hoped, would be waiting for her when she got there.

However, although he had digested Kylie's resumé he still wasn't quite sure what he would get when she arrived. Even if she was one of Australia's top teenage actresses and now a recording artist in her own right, by his own admittance, he had never previously heard of her.

Even though *Neighbours* was enjoying a successful run on British television, it still hadn't reached its height in terms of viewing figures. Reg Watson, the programme's executive producer, was not too concerned, however. He had accumulated enough know-how of television audiences, especially in Britain, to know that a single daily showing at midday was not going to win any awards. It was going to need much more than that – such as being seen during a peak hour time slot.

At that time, of course, Britain was already behind Australia with what had been seen and what hadn't, by almost 18 months, something that would be very much in Kylie's favour in the future; when she would eventually quit *Neighbours*, she was able to make the most of the fact that her character was still seen on UK screens right up to the end of 1989, giving the illusion that she was able to juggle both a music and acting career extremely successfully in the UK. She would have had eight top five UK hit singles, including three Number Ones, plus two Number One albums by the time Charlene disappeared from UK screens.

When Kylie paid that first visit to London, the programme was already encouraging young people to play truant from school – in the middle of the day, with the express purpose of watching *Neighbours*.

'I love the stories I hear about *Neighbours* and just what a phenomenon it was,' Kylie reflected years later in February 2002. 'It's hard for any us that were in the show how to appreciate what was happening at the time. It was just kind of humdrum and hard work doing the show, trying to speed learn your lines within about twenty seconds and then do it and go on to the next scene.'

Although by the end of the year, the viewing figures had grown to 13 million people, despite the less-than-adequate time slot, BBC Television Centre was receiving thousands of letters about those bunking off school. Acknowledging the problem, they agreed – or rather were pressured – to take what steps they could to help.

One of those was to repeat the midday screening with another showing, introduced at the start of the New Year, immediately before the early evening news. Exactly at the time when the young truants, now back at school, had already chosen to chill out between their school and homework.

When Kylie arrived in a damp, cold, typically British autumn, she had every reason to be pleased with herself. She was still seeing Jason despite his insecurities about her flourishing music career. And with 'Locomotion' still selling well, how could she not be? It was also clear at this point that if she had felt that she had been walking in Dannii's shadow, this was also something very firmly in the past. And with her rapidly expanding career, she had more security than ever before. Now financially secure too, her success would even allow her to place the required deposit on her first half-a-million dollar house in Sydney.

Not only that, but her role in *Neighbours* seemed pretty safe and secure for the foreseeable future, particularly in view of its growing popularity with British audiences. But, of course, for the moment *Neighbours* was not her top priority. Kylie was in London with Terry Blamey, hoping to record a follow-up single with Waterman and partners Mike Stock and Matt Aitken. Also collectively known as Stock Aitken Waterman, or SAW.

Between the three of them, they understood the fundamental rules of classic pop music. Probably more than any other producer at that time. Simple chords, irresistible choruses, clear and powerful vocals, lively beat, undemanding lyrics and warm atmospherics. In the previous months and in the years that followed, their danceable pop tunes with programmed drum beats would be dominating the British charts.

The serious music critics, of course, hated their formula-laden music and dippy lyrics, but they sold by the truckload. Perhaps it was that element of their productions that attracted Kylie to collaborate with them in the first place. Today, much of the material that Kylie recorded for them is beginning to be reassessed in terms of being pop classics.

But back in September 1987, all she knew was that if it went according to plan she would be entering another exciting and highly demanding phase of her career. What she didn't realise was that if her life had been hectic up to this point, it was now about to turn into a nightmare.

There were still many hurdles to overcome first though. PWL's managing director David Howells could not track down Pete Waterman, and since he was the only member of the trio who had known that Kylie was coming, she and Terry Blamey were left high and dry in their hotel for a week waiting for a call and wondering, no doubt, what was going on. It was only when they were about to fly back home to Australia that Kylie finally got hauled into their studio to record one of their light pop dance ditties, 'I Should Be So Lucky' which, according to legend, had all but been written in just twenty minutes.

But even with the song written and recorded in Stock Aitken Waterman's London studio, they failed to find a label willing to release the track that had just been laid down. No major record company was in the slightest bit interested. Up until then, SAW's role and function had been purely in recording and production. It was the same for any of the artists they had signed such as Rick Astley and Hazel Dean. They would always be licensed to other labels and record companies.

Not to be discouraged, David Howells, a consummate marketing professional, as well as the managing director of the set-up, was too smart to waste any of Kylie's potential. It was time, he thought, for them to launch their own label. And in late 1987, that's exactly what they did. They released a track by another artist, former model Mandy, to test the waters, but their main concern was Kylie. All involved at PWL were certain they had a massive hit on their hands with 'Lucky', and they weren't about to let the opportunity slip through their fingers.

From that moment, Kylie became part of the new PWL label, and would go on to fund its existence and rapid expansion almost single-handedly. At the same time as much reliance was on the motivation and energy of its employees as on the talent of its artists. Everyone was considered an equal and vital part of the team, whether or not they were a star. Unlike any other operation, artists could be seen brewing coffee and stuffing envelopes as much as they would be making music. Indeed, their biggest selling act at that time, Rick Astley, had joined the PWL stable as a tea boy before he proved his worth as a credible singer.

With the PWL label up and running, and with Kylie back working on *Neighbours* in Melbourne, 'I Should Be So Lucky' was finally released in December 1987. By that time, as the soap was fast gaining millions of British television viewers, the Australian Bicentennial celebrations in Sydney next month would on the 26th be highlighted with an official visit from the Prince and Princess of Wales. Even if such visitations were deplored by some of the more considerable anti-royal groups, Kylie was simply overwhelmed to have had a personal introduction to the celebrated couple.

Charles, not familiar with *Neighbours*, promised Kylie to take steps to fill the gap in his television soap education and would indeed make a point of watching the programme when he returned home. But when it came to speaking with Diana on the same subject, Kylie literally froze on the spot where she stood. Now facing the world's most famous and glamorous woman, the girl from suburban Melbourne whose face was almost as illustrious found all she could do was smile and nod.

'I was going to ask her if she watched the show, but I became a little too nervous and excited,' Kylie would confess later. 'Some people say the royals shouldn't have been there for the celebrations but I disagree. Although I've never been a royal freak, it's an honour to have had them both there.'

And just over a week or two after that, with the British ratings for *Neighbours* still soaring, Kylie's second recording, and first collaboration with SAW's Hit Factory 'I Should Be So Lucky', was simultaneously Number One in the UK and Australia, the first time any artist, male or female, had accomplished such an achievement. And with a six-week run in the pinnacle position in Britain, it became the first gold single of that year.

With *Neighbours* becoming a phenomenal hit on British television and Kylie's topping the charts, she quickly became Fleet Street's new prime target. Acres of column inches were dedicated to these new Australian imports, and along with them came a flurry of ridiculous rumours. One even insisted that Kylie's song did not even feature Kylie's vocals, but instead those of Rick Astley, sped up to sound female.

Kylie, of course, was overwhelmed to be topping the charts, and now not just in her homeland but also halfway across the globe. She refused to be seen to be hurt by any of the tabloid rumours. The constant, insidious nagging that she was being picked on for little reason must have driven her crazy. Whether the rumours were true or not, which of course they weren't, did the world really need to read such rubbish?

Although Kylie did her best to shrug the press attention off, it was the first time in her career that she had had to defend herself against this kind of false gossip. 'They also said I love publicity more than being with my friends,' she eventually snapped. 'As if I would say that.'

Not only would she refuse to appear angry at the stories, but there was no let up in her schedule – it was business as usual. Apart from her daily commitment to filming *Neighbours*, she was now constantly fielding interview requests from around the world because of the success of 'Lucky', which was now hitting the charts throughout much of Europe and would go on to top more than a dozen of them. She was also contractually bound by her new contract with PWL to record a follow-up song and to begin work on her first album for the label. With filming commitments preventing her travelling back to London, Mike Stock flew out to her.

In February they lay down Kylie's vocals in a Melbourne recording studio for two new tracks, the first 'Got To Be Certain' which would become her next single release, and 'Turn It Into Love', a song which, though sadly hidden away on her album, would also mysteriously end up topping the Japanese singles chart for 12 weeks later that year, without the knowledge of PWL.

During these sessions with Mike Stock and his accompanying engineer Karen Hewitt, Kylie, still suffering from the constant pressure of her workload like many would have done in her position, finally broke down into an uncontrollable flood of tears. Although Stock had met Kylie before, five months earlier, he was still shocked to find her in such a state. Naturally, much would be made of Kylie's upset in the press, which labelled it a 'nervous breakdown' rather than the short and much needed release of emotion that Kylie so needed.

Completing only a fraction of the work Stock had intended to get through during his visit, Kylie, together with her mother Carol and Terry Blamey, took another break from *Neighbours* to fly to London that March. When she got off the plane, the press pack was once again waiting for her, and again they were on the attack. This was an entirely new experience for her – the other side of fame that no celebrity enjoys. On top of this, there was even worse press intrusion breaking back home.

A few weeks earlier a young Australian traveller with an eye for golden opportunity had recognised Jason and Kylie in a photograph adorning the wall of a Bali hotel. The picture dated back to their holiday over a year earlier. And to make matters worse, Kylie was topless. When the young traveller sold the picture he had swiped for AU$2,000, practically every newspaper in Australia published it. What was now questionable was how would it affect the wholesome image of *Neighbours,* and what about all those 'Kylie and Jason are just good friends' stories?

Jason already had a stock answer prepared. Every time he was confronted with this, he would simply reinforce his friendship with his co-star by saying that they were on holiday together because they had the same schedule. And that was all there was to it. Most times he won everybody over, but there were still those who probably thought there had to be something going on between them. But the wide publication of the holiday snap from Bali showing Kylie topless failed to make Kylie or Jason admit to anything more.

Outrageous tabloid speculation was now rapidly becoming part and parcel of their success even though they would sometimes use it to camouflage some of the more accurate stories. Another tabloid outburst that appeared in the *Sun* on Kylie's last morning in London, on 4 April 1988, reported that she had been spat at, pushed around and verbally abused by a group of girls in the Hippodrome club in London's West End. It was where, with Pete Waterman, she was doing yet another promotional appearance, and that is where the girls had taken exception to Kylie's fame and apparent fortune.

According to one observer, 'Kylie had only been in the place fifteen minutes when the girls started calling her names and pushing her around. One spat straight in her face. She was badly shaken, but she didn't say a word – just struggled out of her seat and was ushered out. She put on a brave face and even managed a brief smile.' With her dignity more or less intact, she vowed that the story did not contain any truth whatsoever.

By now, she must have been rapidly tiring of enduring the attention of the tabloid press. Emotions only intensified by the knowledge that everybody expected her to be smiling, bubbly, confident and strong. Not that it ended there. On arriving back in Melbourne, she discovered that most of the London stories had spread to Australia, giving the local press there another reason to dig deeper with even more questions, speculation, rumour and gossip.

She had had enough. It had all gone too far. Far more important, Blamey considered, was the need for Kylie to take a break, to get through the next few months with the minimum of stress. Even as she was first tasting international fame, she was probably feeling that she wanted to live a normal teenage life again. Blamey took appropriate action against the media backlash and, for the time being, refused all requests for interviews with Kylie, regardless of the publication. Even some of the biggest UK and Australian magazines and newspapers were turned away.

Blamey was less reticent, of course, when it came to inviting the press in for the 1988 Logie awards. As before, it was another night of triumph for Kylie. She literally scooped the board, winning four awards, an achievement not since equalled by any other actor or actress in the history of the Australian equivalent to the Emmys. Not only was she declared Most Popular Actress for the second year in succession, but also won the much-coveted Golden Logie for Most Popular Personality on Australian Television, while Jason won the Most Popular Actor award.

Blamey was still under fire over his decision to ban any press contact whatsoever with Kylie. He was even accused of getting above himself and encouraging Kylie to do much the same. In fact, all he was doing was looking after his client and acting in her best interests. Not only that, but he was still adapting and familiarising himself with the extraordinary turn of events and circumstances that had now propelled Kylie from soap star to international celebrity.

Perhaps, too, it had got out of hand. Bigger than either he or Kylie had ever imagined. If that is what Blamey thought, then he was right. All the same, insisting once again that his client needed to rest, he sent Kylie to America for the first time for a short holiday and to explore the release of her material for the US market through Geffen Records: David Geffen himself had expressed an interest in taking on Kylie, having viewed several of Kylie's videos.

New York was the ideal setting for Kylie to spend the two-week break from *Neighbours*. She could fade more or less into obscurity and truly relax for the first time since all the craziness had started. It was a place where she could go shopping without fear of being recognised or hounded.

By the time she had returned home from the States, 'I Should Be So Lucky' had unexpectedly become a Number One hit in much of Western Europe – Germany, Israel, Switzerland and Finland – and had also gone Top Five in another half a dozen other territories. It was soon to do similar business across America. And with huge promotional backup from Geffen, it was no wonder. Entering the US charts on the first week of release, the record would eventually climb to peak at Number 28. Quite a remarkable achievement for the first single from an unknown Australian soap star. The only sour note was that, with her rapidly increasing celebrity, she might now have no place left to hide.

But relative normality, and indeed security, beckoned, and once again Kylie was back filming *Neighbours* and making preparations for the release of her second single for PWL, 'Got To Be Certain'. Unaccountably, three different versions of the video were produced.

Two months later, 'Locomotion', now changed to 'The Loco-Motion', had been re-recorded by SAW for both European and US consumption and was being released as Kylie's latest single. It was also the version that appeared on the Australian version of her debut album with Mike Duffy's original version (now considered superior), replaced in favour of the new one. Since then the tape of that original Duffy recording has been stored away in the vaults of Mushroom Records until recently when it was dug out for inclusion on an Australian compilation album of rarities and remixes.

Like Andy Cowan-Martin, then head of artist management at PWL, Kylie was only too aware that success for any artist was partly down to marketing and carefully monitored exposure. For the launch of the new 'Loco-Motion' single, for instance, as with other promotions, it was down to him to get things rolling. One of those occasions was for the dance routine for Kylie's appearance on Terry Wogan's then popular evening television show on the BBC.

'We were not sure how involved Kylie wanted to be in the routine,' Cowan-Martin recalls. 'So I took her to the dance studio to meet the choreographer and the boys. For the first few minutes she just stood and watched them. Then, as if someone had plugged her into the mains supply, she joined in and took the lead. It was a display of complete professionalism and competence. She was a consummate performer.'

And on another occasion, soon after, Cowan-Martin remembers the time when Kylie was scheduled to open a new nerve-racking ride at Alton Towers amusement park – Europe's largest – in Staffordshire. From the early morning call at six o'clock, the party took off from Battersea Heliport three hours later.

'When we landed she underwent her usual transformation from quiet and shy to self-confident pop star, much to the delight of hundreds of adoring fans. It was one of the first times she had been exposed to what can only be called a feeding frenzy of press photographers, all clamouring at once for close-ups. After a briefing we were led out to The Mouse, which Kylie officially opened by taking the first ride, which would scare the pants off any sane person. Then, on the insistence of the press and the PR people, she went round twice more. Terry Blamey didn't seem too concerned, but David Howells and I decided enough was enough and I got her out of there. She looked a little peaky, but despite the ordeal she kept on smiling and signing autographs for the enormous crowds.'

But even then the day was far from over. On the way back to London the chairman of Alton Towers not only diverted the helicopter to his own home to introduce Kylie to his family, but also tried to make it land at other business premises in the area. It was then that Cowan-Martin put his foot down.

'I explained robustly that Kylie had a photo-session in an hour. It later transpired that going round the ride three times had damaged her back. She had to see an osteopath as a result. But she never complained once. A definite trouper.'

Although it was still to be months before she finally succeeded in her struggle to maintain an equilibrium in dealing with such problems and illnesses, and could start enjoying the trappings of fame and celebrity, perhaps she had already figured out what to do about them.

The first indication that she could be on the road to recovery was soon after she returned from America. She broke her self-imposed media silence and talked to the *Melbourne Sun*. In what must have been a great shock to her many fans, she revealed that she was seriously considering leaving *Neighbours* –

the pressures of balancing both a TV and music career were finally getting too much to handle and one of them had to give. True to her resolve, within a month, when she had turned twenty, she filmed her final episode.

In the past, she would have probably relied on Jason to hold her up through the mental anguish she absorbed from the pressure. After all, they had spent the last two years of their lives being supportive to each other above all else – being mates and best friends. But now, it seemed their paths were diverging. Jason had his own manager and was finally chasing the dream to launch his own singing career.

It was back in April, when Kylie was going through the start of her so-called breakdown, that Stock Aitken and Waterman, under some pressure from Mushroom Records, conceded to recording Jason's first record, for release almost six months later. While Australian band Noiseworks had come up with a song for him to cut as a demo at the PWL session in London with Peter Hammond, it would be the SAW track 'Nothing Can Divide Us', originally penned for Rick Astley, that would provide Jason with his first hit.

In fact it was almost ironic that Kylie was now the one with the music career, and yet, looking back, it was Jason who grew up with the musical backdrop. As a child he had been a member of the Australian Boys Choir, and later, as a young man, he played guitar and sang vocals with a variety of bands, always dreaming of a career in rock music.

While Jason was enjoying his first taste of stardom in London that Easter, Kylie was still under pressure. She felt pulled in all different directions by those around her. Gruelling routines were once again taking their toll and endless nights spent preparing for the next day's shooting were just as bad. On top of everything else, she was trying to fit in an ever-expanding schedule of public engagements. No wonder she was exhausted.

At that time, there were only a few outside her own circle who realised just how close she was to complete physical and emotional breakdown. But she was committed to both *Neighbours* and PWL. Even though she later admitted that she went through much of that period in a blur, she didn't know what else she could do. She kept working simply because her contractual commitments didn't offer her any other option, or did they?

Perhaps she knew, deep down, that something had to go. And as far as she was concerned, the clear choice would surely be *Neighbours*. The show's producers had also realised that choice months earlier. It was inevitable that they would soon lose their star.

Although she knew she owed *Neighbours* her loyalty, she eventually gave it up because she couldn't do it justice. If that was true, the producers of *Neighbours* weren't about to let Kylie go without a fight. Casting director Jan Russ, whose vision had given Kylie the opportunity to become part of the phenomenon in the first place, was one of a group of executives who tried to talk her out of quitting but without success.

If the producers were hoping to have support for hanging on to Kylie from Ron Minogue, they were sadly mistaken, even though he apparently held as many reservations about his daughter's leaving as they did. For all its shortfalls, *Neighbours* had provided a reliable and constant source of income, but as for this music industry business? He just wasn't sure. But as on so many other occasions he put Kylie's wishes first and supported her in her decision to leave the series.

Kylie filmed her final scene for *Neighbours* on 10 June 1988. It would also be her final farewell from Ramsay Street. In the show

Charlene would be seen waving goodbye as her car, the little green mini named 'Willy', headed back home to Queensland where her grandfather had given her a house and where she would now live. Even with the matrimonial discord of affairs and upsets that had been introduced in recent months, Scott would follow on soon after. Once he had disentangled himself from his job as a cub reporter with local rag, *The Erinsborough News*.

Filming that last episode, however, was an emotional experience for Kylie. Both on and off the screen, she couldn't control the tears. That evening at a farewell party thrown in her honour at a restaurant in Melbourne, she was again overcome with emotion, and burst into tears three times as she stood up to give thanks for her goodbye gift that the cast and crew had bestowed on her. An antique mirror and farewell card formed from a mosaic of all her promotional pictures.

Despite everyone's best efforts, the press discovered the venue of the secret party and caught up with her when she left the restaurant in the small hours. She knew she had to face them so she did it with good grace.

Perhaps now that it was over, it must have occurred to her, once or twice, to ponder, if only for a moment, whether she was actually doing the right thing.

One of the highlights of *Neighbours* was probably when Russell Crowe was in the show. Now best known for his Oscar-winning role as the Roman general turned slave, Maximus, in Ridley Scott's *Gladiator* and as the mathematician John Nash in Ron Howard's *A Beautiful Mind,* he had appeared in four episodes in 1987 for the simple reason that he wanted to get closer to Kylie.

He remembers, 'I was reading the script and I'm thinking, this is awful. Then I get to the last scene and I've got to punch

Craig McLachlin, and Jason Donovan's trying to break up the fight, while Kylie Minogue is riding on my back trying to strangle me. And I went, yes I'll do it!'

Kylie's last scene as Charlene Mitchell Robinson was still some way off into the future for British television viewers. In fact, it wouldn't be until October the following year. By the time it had been aired in Australia, *Neighbours* was among the most popular programmes in Britain and Scott and Charlene the favourite TV couple.

The impact of Scott and Charlene's wedding was to prove even greater in Britain than it did in Australia. On top of the wealth of press coverage it received, it also turned the Angry Anderson ballad, 'Suddenly', which accompanied the happy couple down the aisle, into a huge hit single. Not only that but Charlene's wedding dress worn by Kylie was also put on display at the Museum of the Moving Image on London's South Bank.

It also led to everything from spoofs on the show's catchy theme tune to earnest discussions about the reason behind the popularity of it all. Exactly why the kids related so strongly to what went on in Ramsay Street is still a mystery. And it didn't take producers long to exploit every opportunity to turn that exact question into television programming to be almost as riveting as the show itself. Studio debates were set up as part of weekend magazine shows aimed at young people, and audience members were encouraged to air their views about what made *Neighbours* such compulsive viewing.

Most times, not surprisingly, the answers came back to Scott and Charlene. For a start, they were just like everyone else, they argued with their parents, and they had problems that they managed to sort out in the end, ran the general consensus. Overall, it seemed that the young folk of Ramsay Street encountered exactly the same obstacles and setbacks as their devoted fans. What is more, they could deal with them. Following plots from day to day was also about discovering that no matter how difficult life is and no matter how rocky the problems – even if most of them feel pretty mountainous to the average 14-year-old – in the end, there is always a solution.

## FIVE

JULY 1988 – NOVEMBER 1989

# COMING OF AGE

Within six months of leaving *Neighbours*, Kylie was to become a true Eighties pop phenomenon. Three of her first six singles would end up at Number One and the other three at Number Two, selling over four million copies. 'I Should Be So Lucky' had already reached the pinnacle position in 18 different countries and her maiden album for PWL would do much the same business by selling two million in Britain and double that around the world. It would even earn her an entry in the *Guinness Book of Records* as the youngest female soloist to have a Number One British album.

By the end of the same year that she had departed Ramsay Street, Kylie had leapt from earning £150 an episode to commanding £10,000 for a personal appearance. She had also sold £25 million worth of records in those twelve months since the beginning of 1988 and probably brought in a personal income of around five million.

It probably helped that she had just returned from a three-month promotional trip across much of the globe to promote her debut album that September, even if she had cut it short due to the exhaustion she was now feeling. But not according to Kylie. She simply put a lot of her success down to luck. 'I realise how incredibly lucky I was to get the part of Charlene. Originally I just thought I was going to be doing the show for twelve weeks. Instead I stayed on for two and a half years.'

And maybe she was right. Certainly luck seemed to have played a part in her good fortune. In January Michael Grade, programme controller at the BBC, bowed to pressure from teenagers who were arriving late to school after watching the morning slot of *Neighbours*. By shifting the show to early evening, he had pulled off the impossible and doubled viewing figures overnight.

Luck played its part again perhaps when Stock Aitken and Waterman agreed to produce her records. Pete Waterman cheerfully admits today that when Kylie and manager Terry Blamey came to meet with him, he had underestimated her popularity. Luck or not, it was that girl-next-door, that 1980s answer to Doris Day, that probably turned Kylie into the daughter that most parents would wish for and the sassy teenager that most adolescent boys would dream of as the perfect match for their first love affair.

But according to David Howells, then managing director of PWL, it was a lot more than that. 'Kylie represents the upside of life,' he says. 'That is the core to her success. She exudes naturalness, fun and enthusiasm. Her qualities are contagious and refreshing. Madonna conveys the all-American, streetwise and raunchy picture. There is no way you could describe Kylie as any of those things.'

Well, not then, anyway.

Waterman agrees. At that time, he said, 'She could be the

biggest female singer of all time. She has a very special talent. She just comes alive the moment she's put in front of a camera or microphone. I've seen her exhausted after a flight, step on stage and be electric. It's the sign of true star quality. The moment she has to perform, wham! It's really quite dazzling.' And once again he was right.

On her return home from that promotional tour, the press was waiting at Melbourne for Kylie's plane to land. Although she was able to put a brave face on things and even explain away with ease her decision to shorten her tour, a couple of days later, having dealt with the media admirably, against all expectations she would announce her love for Jason.

Now that she was no longer in *Neighbours*, she could see no reason at all not to come clean about the fact that they were indeed a couple. As much as the tour she had just cut short, Kylie became equally sick of having to keep up the deception. Going public, she considered, could no longer harm either her own career or Jason's. It was time to spill the beans.

What happened was apparently quite simple. A reporter from *TV Week* had seen the couple out together in a restaurant and, like most journalists, wondered if there was something going on between the pair. When later questioned during one of her regular interviews with the magazine about being spotted, Kylie was quick to respond that, yes, they were seriously dating and had been for some time. They just hadn't admitted it.

'I still take my washing home to Mum and it's nice to have a decent cooked meal every now and then. But I don't live there all the time. I miss being with Jason. That's one of the reasons I don't like going on tour for too long. I really miss him when we're apart.'

It seemed, however, that Kylie's decision to disclose the truth had caused more trouble than she ever thought possible. As before, with the Channel Ten bosses, Mushroom Records were convinced that the secret of their success owed as much to the constant denial of a relationship as to their individual talent.

The best course of action to repair the damage, to keep the myth intact, would be to pretend the interview had never taken place and that Kylie's words were pure invention. If there were ever any questions about it, it was down to some tabloid journalist who had made the whole thing up.

In many ways, it was surprising that Kylie and Jason had even managed to get away with keeping their relationship so secretive for this long. How many more times would journalists and paparazzi have to lay in wait outside Jason's home for any kind of proof that they were indeed a couple and 'Oh my God! Yes, they really are living together'?

But it wasn't simply the tabloid attention that tormented her. Kylie also found herself the victim of something much worse. It was late one night when she was at home in her parent's home.

'I was there alone and there was an intruder in the house. I was in my bedroom. He came in the window and round the bedroom next to mine. And I kind of heard some noises – I was probably playing with my stereo or something. I went to investigate and found these footprints had come in the window and back out. I was chasing this guy – you think you're superhuman – going "I've seen your face, I know who you are."'

Perhaps she thought it was the stalker who had been bombarding her with obscene phone calls and a spate of hate mail; the man who knew where she lived, knew her routine, knew everything about her and made sure she knew he was watching. The man who made simply answering the phone or opening a letter an impossible ordeal.

But the police investigating the break-in at the time believed the intruder was the same one as on their Most Wanted List, following several sex attacks on women around the area where the Minogue home was situated.

Making matters worse as she most probably reflected on the incident was the fact that her relationship with Jason would never be the same again after the *TV Week* fiasco. If anything it would become more like the public perception of it. That they were more friends than lovers.

Even though she agreed to go along with the pretence of not being in a relationship with Jason for the time being, she was probably feeling fragile, a little confused and full of heartache. In her eyes, he had the chance to tell the world how they felt about each other, and he blew it.

So it was perhaps a little strange that the couple agreed, maybe somewhat reluctantly, to record 'Especially For You' as a duet for a release in time for that Christmas. With that decision made as late as November, it was obvious there was little time to waste if PWL were to catch the seasonal market in time for the almost guaranteed hit. It was why Waterman and Matt Aitken organised a flying visit to Melbourne to tape the vocal and returned to London in the space of three days.

Two weeks later, Kylie and Jason would be in London to perform the track live at the Children's Royal Variety Show in the presence of Princess Margaret, Prince William and Prince Harry. Strangely enough, considering how Kylie was feeling about Jason, they also enjoyed a week of secret passion (according to the *Daily Mirror*) at the Pembridge Court Hotel, just off

Portobello Road, paying one hundred pounds a night for their deluxe honeymoon suite.

> To try and keep the gossip at bay they even took along Kylie's brother Brendan as a chaperone but he roughed it in a single room down the hall [said the *Mirror*]. They are a secretive couple and keep out of sight. They have taken one of the rooms usually let to married couples and have been enjoying the luxury of breakfast in bed. They are rarely seen out of the room and when the chauffeur arrives, they always make a dash for it. Jason even sneaks out the back door.

Whether that was true or not, just over a month later, by which time the New Year celebrations had passed, it looked like Kylie had made a concious decision to change herself. Determined to change, she first threw herself into her work schedule and then, with terrifying resolve, insisted on having weekends off. Previously she may have gone along with the 14-hour days and the seven-day weeks, but not any more.

Jason, too, loved the new Kylie. But, of course, he was basking in the glow of his own new career as a pop icon. His album, *Ten Good Reasons*, had already raced to the Number One position in the UK, and although he and PWL were making the most of their new-found success, perhaps he had overlooked the fact that sharing his life with Kylie may have been coming to an end.

For Kylie, the previous year had ended on a large dose of grim reality. In her eyes, quite rightly, she thought that Jason had let her down badly, and perhaps now she found that she was unable to have the same feelings towards him. Although they would still share the same house any time they were in Australia, or an apartment in London, they weren't in either place that much. Not together anyway.

And that was how they would spend much of their time: sometimes together, sometimes on their own, either on a plane, in a car, or at a hotel for the night whenever their schedules came together, probably two or three times a month, if that. So while they were drifting apart because of Jason's behaviour, the demands of their careers made it harder for them to be reconciled.

Kylie wasn't worried. With the help of Sydney-based stylist, Nicole Bonython, she had already shed the careless, slightly unkempt image she had cultivated in the Charlene days, the riot of blonde curls had been tamed, and even in jeans, fluffy jumper and T-shirt, she had acquired a gloss of sophistication.

Perhaps that was something to do with the fact that she had just landed her first starring role in a feature film. Although it had been achieved with the help of a Los Angeles-based agent, it was something she had long wanted to do. Terry Blamey, working in her interests, had looked at a great number of scripts during the previous year and turned them all down, deeming most as unsuitable. Even after leaving *Neighbours*, there had been talk of another television mini-series alongside a cast of star names, but that's where the talk ended. Blamey persevered, and finally at the end of the year, he came up trumps with a project that he believed would be perfect for Kylie. And it was.

*The Delinquents* was based on a 1960s novel by Australian author Deirdre Cash and could best be described as a rites of passage story charting eight formative years in the young life of country girl Lola Lovell as she shook free the shackles of authority that surrounded her.

Set in the Teddy Boy era of the Fifties, it was the brainchild of Australian film producers Mike Wilcox and Alex Cutler who had acquired the film rights to the book in the mid-1980s when they were still up-and-coming in their respective fields of film-making. Established and confident years later, their idea to turn the book into a movie remained unabated, even though they'd been trying to place the project with a studio, but without success for as long as they could remember. In fact, it wasn't until rock star David Bowie expressed an interest that the project started to attract attention from some of the big league studios.

Even if Bowie had withdrawn his interest before filming got under way in Queensland in early May, over what he later expressed disdain at the now watered-down version of the book the movie had become, it still attracted the attention of Hollywood giants, Warner Brothers. That was when Village Roadshow, the company's Australian distribution subsidiary, agreed to bankroll the production on the condition that Kylie Minogue, then Australia's hottest property, could be recruited to play the lead role. Even though the two producers had considered Nicole Kidman as a possibility, it was indeed Kylie whom they really wanted for the role of Lola Lovell.

Kylie was equally enthusiastic. 'It did take a while to find the right script. I was getting sent a lot of scripts from people who just wanted to have my name there to sell it at the box office. As an actress, I wanted something completely different to Charlene and something that would be a challenge for me. It's important for me that I continue to grow as an actress.' And *The Delinquents* it seemed would offer her that opportunity.

There would, however, be one disappointment for Ben Mendelsohn, Kylie's old ally from *The Henderson Kids* and *Fame and Fortune*. Although he had already been cast in the role of

Brownie Hanson, Kylie's love interest, he would ultimately be replaced for no other reason than Warner's wanted an American actor. That actor, it turned out would be Charlie Schlatter, best known at the time for *18 Again, Heartbreak Hotel,* and probably most significantly, for playing Michael J Fox's little brother in *Brights Lights, Big City.*

News of the production was officially announced at a Sydney press conference towards the end of April in 1989, almost one month to the day before Kylie's 21st birthday. It was here that both Kylie and Schlatter were introduced to the international media to answer questions about the forthcoming movie.

The character of Lola, a rebellious but passionate teenager with a finger on the self-destruct button was light years away from the uncorrupted, naive girl mechanic from Ramsay Street that Kylie had played in *Neighbours.* Unsurprisingly therefore, the hot topic that every journalist wanted to ask was how would her fans react to her changing from sweet, innocent, squeaky-clean Kylie to this girl who has sex, an abortion and smokes. And would she be baring herself on film? This must have been very frustrating for Kylie, who obviously wanted to focus on her acting ability and the progression of her career.

Filming began in a quiet Queensland town called Maryborough which became home for a while for Kylie annd Schlatter. Even though the locals were probably fascinated by the frenetic energy of the crew and cast around, perhaps they also wondered why nothing seemed to be happening.

Like any movie in production, scenes that were laboriously set up over hours of preparation would be cut short or removed with barely a word and the order of shooting would bare no resemblance to the sequence of the storyline in the script. Neither would the curious crowds that gathered day after day have known anything about film language: rolling, speed, slate, action. To them, the world of cinema must have appeared as confusing and distracting at best. And then there were the paparazzi, gathering like vultures for their world exclusives.

Upset at the time, Kylie laughs today. 'We turned it into a game, trying to spot the photographers hiding all over the place. They were up trees or in a building nearby. I can't stop any of that. You can't get rid of them but I know how to stand up for myself now.'

She was also being accorded the kind of professional respect she had never known before. She would be asked for her input and opinion throughout the time the project was in production; to consider, among other things, every single gesture she made to the camera. Unlike working on *Neighbours*, here it didn't really matter if it took an entire day to get a scene exactly right.

'In film every line is important so you just don't waffle over it,' Kylie explains. 'You're trying to shape your character. You have to be precise. In a series like *Neighbours*, you just talk all the time. Someone has to be coming in the back door or something has to be happening. In film, it's like two or three months so you really put everything into it for that time.

'Everyone is very dedicated. But in a series, if there's some-one you don't like, you have to live with them and you can get quite angry. It gets monotonous and it can be very boring and you go stale. I liked the fact that in the film, the character had a beginning and an end. You could see where the character was going. But in a series, you don't now what's going to happen so it's harder, I think.'

Not only that, but her enthusiasm and natural ability to soak up information and instruction impressed everyone. As director Chris Thomson noted, 'Kylie is an extraordinary actress. I knew she was going to be good when we first started rehearsing, but I honestly didn't know she was going to be this good. I didn't realise at first the strength of her determination and ambition to be an actress. The only time she was ever irritable was with herself, whenever she didn't get something right on the first take.'

Producer Alex Cutler agreed. 'She is a consummate professional and as well as lighting up the screen whenever she appears, she also has that indefinable quality that compels you to watch her. Whatever *it* is – she's got it.'

As if any further proof of this was needed, as they began filming Kylie heard that 'Hand on Your Heart' had reached Number One in England. It was her third in the last 16 months.

Three weeks later, during one of her brief treks home to Melbourne, Kylie had flown a thousand miles for the £50,000 bash that would mark the celebration of her 21st for over a hundred friends and acquaintances gathered at the Red Eagle, the smart, glitzy hotel on the beachfront.

From the airport she was whisked away by Terry Blamey to join Jason. They journeyed to the party together in a white Mercedes. 'The people most important to me are here,' she said at the time. She would return just one week later to celebrate Jason's coming of age, but according to observers, neither party gave her as much pleasure as the impromptu bash thrown for her on the set of *The Delinquents*.

In fact, Kylie had such a good time in that first month of filming that, compared to the frenetic pace of the last few years, she considered it quite a pleasure. Her mother Carol Minogue was always around on set, and even though Jason did travel back and forth to see her whenever he could, didn't stay around for that long. His life, too, was now as hectic as Kylie's.

She had leaped into her new role as a movie actress without hesitation and was sad when it came to an end in June 1989. It had obviously strengthened her confidence and self-esteem; further evidence for this can be seen in two other events which changed the way she thought at around that time.

More than a year on from Charlene's departure from Ramsay Street, Grundy Independent Television Productions were eager to continue milking the rampant success of their top-rated soap. They asked Kylie for permission for the commercial release of a 90-minute compilation video entitled *Scott and Charlene: A Love Story*. But Kylie, now anxious to move on and place *Neighbours* firmly in her past, turned down the permission that Grundy were seeking. But much to her amazement, they planned to release it anyway.

When Kylie left *Neighbours,* she had been only too pleased to acknowledge the debt she felt she owed the programme, and even though the storyline was left open for her to return at any time to Ramsay Street, by the following year things had changed dramatically as far as her career was concerned. Understandably she didn't want to be forever associated with her character, Charlene Mitchell.

As her lawyers pointed out in her bid to stop the video being issued, she had taken great pains to develop a career as a sophisticated singer, and if the video was indeed put out, Kylie felt her new career would be significantly and adversely affected.

Even though her attempts failed to prevent the video being released, she was right, of course. As far as she was concerned, Scott and Charlene were now well and truly a thing of the past, or at least, they were in Australia: it would be some months yet before the rest of the world had caught up. Britain, for instance, was still a long way behind. Viewers would not see the last of Charlene until early November 1989. Perhaps that on its own was a relief to Kylie. And if she was still feeling annoyed at the decision of Grundy's to release that video, perhaps there was more satisfaction to be had out of the fact that without Charlene, without Kylie, *Neighbours* would finally fall from grace in the television ratings war.

Within a fortnight of her work being completed on *The Delinquents* just two months after it had started, Kylie again took off for London to start work on her second album *Enjoy Yourself* for Stock Aitken Waterman.

It also marked the beginning of the end of her association with SAW. Certainly up to that point, Kylie's new music was still being created in much the same manner that was used on all her previous recordings, and indeed for most other artists signed to the PWL stable.

All the same, just three weeks after Kylie had arrived in London, the tracks needed to fill the album had been completed. It was at the end of those sessions that Kylie's seventh single, 'Wouldn't Change A Thing', would, as pretty much expected, enter the UK chart at Number Two.

Jason, too, was having similar success with his album *Ten Good Reasons*. But by then, of course, Kylie and Jason had become more estranged from each other than ever before. They were spending more time, without each other, on opposite sides of the globe. Yet, the previous year, when Kylie had cut short her promotional tour, one of the reasons she did so was so that she could return home to be with Jason. But now, as she embarked on a 14-date road show of live appearances leading up to the release of *Enjoy Yourself*, she had every intention of staying the course. She also quickly discovered that she could survive without Jason by her side, and without his support.

All the same, says Kylie, 'It can get lonely because you go out and you may be making all these thousands of people happy and then you get back to your hotel room and you're completely on your own. It's usually too late to go out and because of the time difference it's often hard to call home. So you can be pretty lonely and that's where a support group is necessary. It sounds like therapy, but there's my manager, my assistant and friends, who are especially important. Friends who understand what I do. It's great if one of my girlfriends or my mum and Dannii can travel with me. I really enjoy that.'

It was obvious that it wouldn't be too long before a new involvement with someone else would beckon, but it happened sooner than expected. Back in July 1987, when she had met Michael Hutchence, it was only for a brief, spellbound moment. As lead vocalist of INXS, Australia's leading maverick rock band, Hutchence was already a huge star and at the *Countdown* music awards in Sydney, he had caught her completely off-guard.

With Jason being a huge fan of the band, it was pretty obvious that he and Kylie would catch their concert at Melbourne. Two years after Kylie's first encounter with Hutchence, they were invited back to the after-show party at the band's inner-city hotel. Jason, of course, was in his element. What could possibly have been better than wrapping up the evening indulging in his favourite habit and, even better, with one of his idols?

But perhaps what Jason failed to realise as he became more stoned as the night wore on was that his idol was making a play for his girlfriend. Even though Michael, like most, had at one time or another given Kylie some bad times in the press, he wanted to apologise, or at least that's what he told her. But, of course, he had his sights set much higher than merely mending broken fences. Simply put, he wanted to do with her what he had vociferously expressed at the *Countdown* awards. That moment when he was running towards her shouting, 'I want to fuck you, I want to fuck you.'

And here, at the end of 1989, he could perhaps seize the opportunity to do something about it.

## SIX

## DECEMBER 1989 – DECEMBER 1990

# A DANGEROUS ADDICTION

By Christmas 1989, Kylie was with Michael Hutchence although his seduction of Kylie really began in September. That was when Kylie, with her mother Carol, and manager Terry Blamey, arrived in Hong Kong en route to the the start of her first ever live tour. Supported by Sinitta and Pete Burns from Dead Or Alive, the show would open on 2 October in Nagoya, Japan's third largest city, playing four shows to over 40,000 Japanese fans under the name of 'Disco in Dreams' before heading off to the UK to open at London's Hammersmith Palais followed by another nine dates from Bristol to Birmingham.

The UK was where the tour with the same set list, minus Sinitta and Burns and instead accompanied by several other acts from the PWL stable, became part of 'The Hitman Roadshow' with giveaway tickets through radio, television and print media, similar to the one headlined by Jason the previous year.

'It was really fantastic,' said Kylie. 'It was great to give myself totally to my public. The crowd was very receptive, especially in Osaka, were the stage was close to the audience. I was a little nervous before going on in Tokyo but I said to myself, let's do it and forget there are so many people out there.'

Even if Pete Waterman was slightly concerned before the start of the tour, his fears were soon shaken off. 'We were a bit worried that with Kylie we might not get the adulation we got for Jason's tour, but by golly, we have. We're getting the same reaction, but just a bit louder. I can't think of a time, and I've been doing this since 1967, when girls have screamed at another girl like this. That's a new phenomenon.'

During the weeks prior to her arrival in Hong Kong, she had been in rehearsal in London with her four dancers; Venol John, Richard Allen, Paul Smith and Kevan Allen; and without a band, the back-up tapes she would sing live to. She had arrived early in Hong Kong to take in a guest appearance at the Miss Asia-Pacific beauty contest and to grab a short break before the tour opened. It just so happened that Hong Kong was also where Michael Hutchence was living at the time – not that surprisingly since it was the city in which he had been raised as a child.

Born in Sydney, Australia on 22 January 1960 to fashion dealer Kelland Hutchence and his make-up artist wife Patricia, he was just four when the family moved to Hong Kong, growing up in what would best be described as an unconventional upbringing.

When he was twelve, they went back to the Sydney suburb of Davidson. Three years later, when his parents divorced, he moved with his mother to Los Angeles where he stayed for about a year until he had enough money saved to return home again. Soon after he did, along with some friends, he formed the band that would eventually become INXS – on 16 August 1977, the day that the other original bad boy of rock, Elvis Presley died.

When Kylie had arrived in Hong Kong, Hutchence, already having shown an interest in her, decided that she might be fun to pursue. On meeting her, despite his 'wild man of rock' image, he was the perfect gentleman. And little did Kylie's entourage know but she had, in fact, already agreed to meet up with him.

According to Vincent Lovegrove's 1999 biography of Hutchence, Kylie had told Michael she was going to be in Hong Kong. 'He said he would be there too and offered to take me out,' Kylie told the author. 'What I didn't know was that he'd been told I was coming and had travelled to Hong Kong specially.'

The next evening, Kylie waited and waited for Michael to pick her up. He was three hours late. 'But we went out,' she continues. 'And must have stayed out talking in the streets of Hong Kong till four or five in the morning. We just hit it off amazingly well. But I wouldn't let him kiss me, which probably drove him crazy. After that, he started sending flowers and there were constant phone calls. Then we started going out. I just remember him treating me so well. He did throughout out entire relationship.'

Whatever the correct sequence of events, Kylie had never enjoyed herself so much. Michael was literally knocked out with her as much as she was with him. If there had never been anything quite as comparable to the feelings he felt he had for Kylie, then before she left the city, he made damn sure she knew what his intentions were. He wanted her as his new lover.

'I used to be a Kylie knocker, hated what she stood for, never watched *Neighbours*,' he said at the time. 'She's very underestimated. She's not at all this wimpish personality people think she is. She's very intelligent and deep.'

With his new found admiration for Kylie in mind, Michael sought her out again a week later, on 6 October, on the night Kylie's tour had reached Toyko. He suggested a night out clubbing. She accepted. And with the other 12 or so people in her entourage they headed to the club Michael had in mind.

Michael had badly wanted to kiss her the last time they'd gone out, but this time he made do with just trying to hold her hand. She wouldn't even let him do that, pushing him away every time he made an attempt. But he wore her down and by the end of the evening, and now feeling very comfortable in his company, she relented enough to walk with him arm in arm.

'I'm a fatalist,' says Kylie in retrospect. 'That was the time I was meant to meet him. It was like my blinkers were taken off and I entered the next stage. I was a surburban girl working in a soap opera, and it was like "Wow! Oh my God!" I was too naive to think why he would be interested in me. I was meant to blossom a bit and learn a bit about the world. And I can't think of a better person to do it with.'

Kylie and Michael packed a great deal into the next few days. Not that they had much time to prolong the joy of it right then. Kylie's first British show, at London's Hammersmith Palais on 15 October made sure of that. All the same they made plans to meet again in Hong Kong when her tour had ended. It was a promise she would find no difficulty in keeping. And by the time the couple returned to Australia that November 1989, after they had spent a week together at the end of the tour, some areas of the media were stating that it was clear that Kylie was now a completely different person, that she had been awakened in every way possible, sexually, musically, in appearance and in self-confidence. And Michael did all of that.

Kylie, years later, commented that she found this 'moulded

by a boyfriend' theory quite offensive. 'I was really annoyed about that and I think I went to great lengths to assure them that it wasn't the case. It's not that shallow a situation, is it? I agree with it in some ways, but I'm not moulded by anyone I go out with. I have my own thoughts, actions and feelings, haven't I? If anyone's in love they obviously begin to think and act in a sympathetic way to their partner – it's give and take. That's what love's all about.'

However, even though Kylie maintains she never said her most famous quote about Michael helping her to discover sex, years later she would laugh and admit that even if she had not uttered the words, they were true. 'He was totally charismatic and intelligent, witty, funny and filthy.'

'Let's just say Hutch opened my eyes to the ways of the world that I had not yet experienced.'

One of those times, she remembers, was when he encouraged her with her image and live performances, always paying attention to her career. 'I remember doing a secret warm-up gig in a small club. I was nervous but he was so proud of me. He took a back seat and let me shine.'

All the same, it appeared that sex was their cornerstone. Michael often boasted to friends that 'Kylie was the best fuck in the world.' Certainly, Kylie said, 'There was just this electric sexual energy between us. Even after we finished, people would say "Oh my God, you two." We could be on opposite sides of the room and I could see his eyes. I can still see them right now.'

To many, Michael Hutchence had literally turned Kylie on her head. It was the wildest transformation one was ever likely to see. Within weeks, it was an immediate, instant change, and it was obvious to anyone interested enough to observe. 'Michael encouraged me to be myself,' she says.

For the first time, Kylie could speak openly about a relation-ship without fear of reprisal. Everyone who had known about Jason had gone along with the smokescreen, but now she could let her guard down. It was fine to tell the truth. Even if she did, for a while keep up the 'just good friends' line that continued to crop up in interviews. For instance, at a press conference return-ing to Sydney, she was able to say that they had dated a couple of times and that Michael was different from how people imagined him: 'He's really impressive – he's deep, sometimes.'

Eventually, of course, she wouldn't need to be so protective any more and even hinted at the possibility that children might be part of their future plans, even if marriage wasn't. 'It sounds like I'm a complete hippie but I have found myself more. It's a sense of self and a sense of direction and, because of that, I'm really looking forward to the future.' Suddenly Kylie was speaking out, speaking her mind, without a script.

Kylie's new 'expect the unexpected' attitude was all-embrac-ing. Adapting quickly to her new environment and Michael's circle of friends, things were changing quite dramatically over the coming weeks and months. Formerly a wide-eyed teenage actress, suddenly she emerged, decked out in blonde wigs and mini-skirts, a sultry, sensual woman in full command of her public persona. It was obvious that their love affair was proving a boost to both their careers and further enhancing Michael's sexual reputation. In short they were the coolest couple around. And if there was one thing Kylie had wanted to be thought of, it was cool.

'I was 21 when I started dating Michael and I've always said that it was like I had blinkers taken on and then I took them off. We went out for about 18 months, but it seemed a lot longer. It was very intense and wonderful and it drove my manager crazy, because Michael and I used to meet all over the place. I used to get my manager to shimmy things along so I could go to Frankfurt for the weekend, then fly off to Hong Kong.'

Not so cool, however, was the initial news of Kylie's new relationship among her family who were very shocked. They were, however, pleasantly surprised when they met him.

Indeed, when they lost contact with her for a week they went frantic with worry. They were probably concerned because Michael would have probably introduced Kylie to partying, drinking and drugs. And as he had never made a secret of his fondness for any of them, there would be every reason to think the worst. Most certainly, he would have probably tried to convince Kylie that a bit of dope or an ecstasy tablet wouldn't kill her, though later she revealed that she had only experimented with ecstasy.

But then again, her views on drugs did sometimes appear contradictory: 'It can be fun and it can be dangerous,' she once told a journalist. 'I'm all for kids not taking drugs. But I don't want to say to them you should never try anything. You have to experience something new to have a view on it.' Later, of course, she would change her stance completely. 'Some things you can only talk about if you've had experience, but I would condemn drugs now.' At the time, however, reports on her comments on drug use even had the Australian Parliament involved.

'I did some interviews before I left Australia,' she remembers, 'and one of them was for a colour supplement for some paper over there. The guy asked me about drugs and I said, "Well, I'm not going to talk to you about me and drugs," and something like, "I don't want to tell people not to take drugs." My whole point in the article was that I don't want to be wagging my finger at kids saying, "Oh no, you shouldn't be doing this," because kids get that the whole time and besides they're more educated today than they've ever been, so you should be able to talk openly about things. Anyway, these comments were taken literally and some politician took issue with it in Parliament you know, saying "Pop stars should be more responsible" and I was over here going crazy thinking, "My God, what's going on?" I had to issue a counter statement and everything.

'My views are a lot deeper than five sentences on a piece of paper, y'know. I try to be careful what I say but I want to be honest with it. What I do in my time I don't talk about and whatever I do in my own house is my own business anyway.'

But then Kylie never really had a chance to rebel like most other teenagers. Since the age of eleven she had literally grown up in front of the camera or spent most of her 'wild' youth in the flashbulbs of paparazzi. So, maybe Michael was just showing her that being bad was not actually so bad. That breaking a few golden rules now and then could also be fun. She couldn't always be worrying that every little move she made would affect her career.

'If you're having a good relationship you can expect to be affected in all sorts of ways,' Kylie commented at the time. 'For too long my kind of relationships were mixed in with work and I really didn't know where the line was. Now I'm in a position where I can step back and say this is work, this is my relationship.'

He was also equally amazed by what she told him about the punishing work schedule she endured. When he heard what she had had to say he encouraged her to stand up for herself and have things done the way she wanted. After all, she was the star. His attitude to fame was like nothing she had ever encountered: a demanding and self-centred approach, which of course, added even more allure to his personality.

It was as if Kylie was completing an 11-year cycle. When she was just ten, she had watched Olivia Newton-John in the movie

*Grease* take a giant step as the naive, self-effacing adolescent in gingham and frills metamorphosed into an up-front assertive young woman in black leather. Now, aged 21, she too was shedding the metaphorical gingham and donning the black leather.

The influence wasn't all one-way. While much was made of how Hutchence had 'corrupted' Kylie, noboday talked about how she calmed him down and softened some of his rock 'n' roll excesses. It wasn't very newsworthy to report that they did things that any normal couple do: hanging out with friends, going for walks, trips on his motorcycle, or relaxing in a park.

Until one such innocent pastime proved far more risky than any of their more hazardous pursuits. On one occasion a photographer was stalking them as they spent time together in a park in Sydney. The first the couple would know of it was when the photographs found their way into magazines in Australia and England. It might not have been so bad, except that one showed Kylie in her underwear intimately embracing Michael.

Michael, not used to such media intrusion on his private life was absolutely furious. But dealing with media intrusion was probably the one thing that Kylie could teach Michael.

Kylie was given precious little time to register a backlash, however. She now had to fit her work around play as much as she could. She was, after all, still promoting the *Enjoy Yourself* album, and now that Charlene had finally left Ramsay Street in Britain as well, and with speculation running high about her popularity being on the wane, she couldn't ignore the demands on her time. Once again, she was off and running an another hectic round of public engagements and personal appearances.

Among them was a song and dance routine she performed with Des O'Connor on his weekly TV show. On top of that, she recorded a video that also ended up as a Christmas Eve Special on ITV called *Kylie on the Go* that was, in fact, the 'Disco In Dreams' show with backstage footage and various clips of Kylie around Japan. And if that wasn't enough, she even found time to pose for her official 1990 Kylie calendar which, throughout the 12 full-page pictures, would premier her new, sultry, grown-up look in a Madonna-style strappy dress, a revealing tie-front cowboy shirt, striped leggings and a sparkly black top.

Not only that but she also walked the red carpet in Regent Street to switch on the London Christmas lights, following in the footsteps of such notables as Princess Diana and Joan Collins. Tens of thousands of young fans carrying 'We Love You' placards waited two hours in very cold weather for Kylie to arrive. People were stretched out for half-a-mile in each direction, giving police the usual nightmare of restraining the onlookers behind barricades.

'I'm honoured to be following in the steps of royalty and Dame Edna,' she told the shivering crowd. 'Well, she is the closest thing Australia has to a queen,' she joked. But afterwards, she admitted to knowing how the Queen must have felt at such occasions. 'It's hard to explain to people what it's like when all you can do is wave – you feel really stupid.'

Four days later, the streets of London were again brought to a standstill for the world premiere of *The Delinquents* at the Warner cinema in Leicester Square when Kylie turned up twenty minutes earlier than she should have. Stepping out of a Fifties-style soft-top Cadillac with Terry Blamey, and dressed in a sophisticated see-through gown slashed to the waist to show off a pair of beaded black hot pants, but without Michael by her side, it was Jason who made the grand entrance during the official guest arrivals on the arm of Texan model Denise Lewis.

It was probably the first time that Jason and Kylie had clapped eyes on each other since their high-profile appearances at the *Smash Hits* readers' poll awards two months earlier. The same month, in fact, that she broke up with him during a transatlantic telephone conversation they had while he was in New York.

But they had, of course, already come across each other at the recording session of *Do They Know It's Christmas* for Band Aid II – a project designed to raise funds for famine in Ethiopia. The track was recorded at PWL over two days in early December with other artists such as Cliff Richard, Banararama, Big Fun, Bros, Chris Rea, Jimmy Sommerville, Sonia and Lisa Stansfield also contributing vocals, with Kylie singing the famous opening line originally performed by Paul Young.

Shortly after that Kylie and Michael would very publicly announce their relationship by their dramatic arrival at the Australian premiere for *The Delinquents*. With Kylie wearing a short blonde wig and a noughts and crosses glittering mini-dress, the awaiting paparazzi were momentarily unaware of who the charismatic couple arriving on the Harley Davidson motorcycle actually were, but it didn't take them long to figure it out. Something else they remained unaware of was the reason for Kylie's surprisingly early departure from the function – not to be cool or aloof, but because the wig she was wearing was a size too small and was giving her a migraine. All the same, the event hit the headlines and was splashed across TV and radio throughout Australia.

A few days later, Kylie and Michael found themselves back in her familiar world of Melbourne to spend Christmas with her family and prepare for her first all-live concerts. And then in the New Year's Eve *Review of the Decade* for the BBC she received yet another accolade, in a year which had brought new success, new experiences and new love, Clive James, Australia's leading humorist and observer of human nature, nominated her as 'Woman of the Decade'.

With holidays out the way, Kylie quickly kicked into the preparations for her debut concerts with a live backing band. There would be three venues in all. The Brisbane Entertainment Centre on 3 February, followed by two more in Sydney and Melbourne. Perhaps it was strange to some that since her music career had started, Kylie had largely shied away from the idea of performing live. But she had her reasons. 'I was determined not to give in to any pressure to perform before I was ready.' Not that her music really needed any extra exposure anyway. The only difference now maybe was that she felt that she was ready to take on the challenge.

The recent 'Hitman Roadshow' tour had played to 170,000 people in the UK alone, and was really more of a promotional outing than anything else, but it was enough to provide Kylie with the extra push she needed to go ahead with a tour. Even so, she still remained somewhat anxious of how it might turn out. She was only too aware that the idea, no matter how much it appealed, was still a risk.

'It's really putting myself out to be either raised up or thrown sticks at, but that's what this whole business is about. It's pretty scary putting yourself out there but you'll never learn if you never take the plunge.'

Once the decision had been made, however, it was down to Terry Blamey to organise an eight-piece band out of his cabaret contacts in Melbourne. Even if Kylie's musical tastes had changed dramatically along with everything else during her first few months with Michael, his musical influences wouldn't have much bearing for the material she would choose for her forthcoming live shows. She did give surprisingly competent renditions of 'Blame It On the Boogie', 'ABC' and 'Dance To The Music', elements of the show which prompted critics to comment on her new found confidence on stage. Much of the show, however, would be based on what she had filled her first two albums with, as well as her current hit single, 'Tears On My Pillow' from the soundtrack of *The Delinquents*. Like most of its predecessors, the single had stormed into the British charts at Number Two, before landing at the pinnacle position the following week.

If there was anything of Michael's influence, it would be in the choice of musicians that she wanted for the final line-up of her band. Both percussionist Greg Perano from the underground rock band The Deadly Hume and bass player James Freud were old buddies of Michael's from gigs that both he and Kylie had regularly attended over the last few weeks.

Freud in many ways seemed a peculiar choice. He was not a natural stablemate for a protégé of Stock Aitken Waterman. He despised the ethos they had created and disparaged their single-mindedly commercial attitude which, he claimed, encouraged young record buyers to buy bandwagon music instead of allowing their taste to develop.

With her band complete, and Kylie having spent much of the early part of the year in Melbourne rehearsing, she had still considered that a warm-up gig would be a good idea. The concert took place at the Cadillac Bar in Melbourne on 29 January and to ensure that not too many people found out about it they were billed as The Singing Budgies.

When the tour opened proper, many of her audience on the opening night at Brisbane and at the other two shows were pre-teen, dressed in cute miniskirts or fringed shorts, reminiscent of a previous Kylie incarnation, but attendances at each venue still topped 10,000.

Kylie, on the other hand, turned out in a slinky black velvet catsuit and matching floppy hat, looked simply dazzling. Even the reviewers, usually ready to express objection, declared themselves surprised to find that she could not only sing and dance but do both together – and very well into the bargain. In her hometown of Melbourne, where critics had always taken her to their hearts, there was a note of even greater triumph in their reviews. 'It's time to ditch the snobbery and face facts – the kid's a star.'

A week before the warm-up gig, Kylie had made one of her regular trips to Sydney to be with Michael to help him celebrate his 30th birthday. Not only that but she personally assisted in organising the whole thing at an inner-city warehouse. It was attended by over 200 of Michael's friends, including members of his own band, Kylie's sister Dannii and Hollywood star Billy Zane – all of whom had gathered to celebrate the occasion in style.

Even so, their time together was now becoming precious. Within days of Kylie's Australian tour ending, and obviously feeling pleased with her own performances, she immediately announced that she was extending the tour to take in the UK, Europe and Asia through April and May.

For the moment though, she could at least return to spending as much time as she could with Michael. He was still in Sydney working on the next INXS album, ultimately to be called X. But they both knew that they would be spending more time apart than together in the months that followed.

One of those times apart was in the middle of March, by which time Kylie was sharing a rented apartment with Terry Blamey in Hollywood. The two had gone to Los Angeles to enable

Kylie to work with some different record producers while Blamey could hunt around for prospective movie projects.

But on arrival in Los Angeles, Kylie was devastated when an opportunist airport thief snatched her handbag and, with it, a collection of holiday photographs and some letters Michael had written to her during their separations. Not only did they have great sentimental value, especially now that they were apart yet again, but there was also the concern that they might fall into wrong hands, resulting in another invasion of her and Michael's privacy.

In the end, no such repercussions would come out of the incident, aside from making her feel very uneasy, but her work in America soon took precedence in her mind. For Kylie, the main purpose of the trip was to enlist the help of some prestigious music producers. Stephen Bray was one. He had co-written 'Into The Groove' and 'Express Yourself' for Madonna. The other two were Paula Abdul producer Keith Cohen and Martika producer Michael Jay. And all had reputations that preceded them.

With such an array of talent, it's not surprising that four tracks from this session ended up on her next album. The best way to describe her American work would be as collaboration. 'That's something I hadn't done before,' Kylie explains. 'With SAW songs, I heard them the day I recorded them, sometimes two songs in a day. I have to be careful not to make PWL sound like an absolute nightmare but to work on a song, demo it and live with it for a while is bliss and a much longer process than what I'm used to.'

Kylie would even dedicate one of the songs she recorded, 'Count The Days', to Michael. 'That's about being away from each other because it's obviously difficult for us to match up – we're both so busy.' Michael, of course, had already written one for her.

It was called 'Suicide Blonde'. And years later he could still recall the inspiration for the song, which would top the charts around the world by the end of the year, ironically, when their relationship was already said to be on the rocks.

'Kylie dyed her hair this colour she called suicide blonde. She said, "I'm going to go suicide blonde today." I think she was thinking of people like Marilyn Monroe and I thought it was a good name, especially as Madonna was big at the time.'

Not long after the LA sessions, it was time to get the show on the road once more – Kylie was touring again.

Among the catalogue of hits performed on the Australian leg of the tour was a new track, 'Better The Devil You Know', which was to become her next release. The song took Kylie in a new direction, more edgy, more dancey, and performed by Kylie with a new-found energy. This was more than another Hit Factory pop ditty. The song would become yet another smash hit, and go on to become the all time fans' favourite, *the* 'Kylie Classic'. The lyrics were touted by many as SAW's best yet by far. Years later, Pete Waterman would admit that SAW had written the song about Kylie's relationship with Jason. Like many, they thought her being with Michael was just too risky.

But Kylie didn't care. Having recorded the track in a mad rush in London during March 1990, she probably hadn't even been aware of the meaning to the song, and was straight back into rehearsals and running up huge telephone bills speaking to Michael back home in Australia.

It was an exhausting tour but also a rewarding one – highlights included Kylie singing at the John Lennon Memorial Concert in Liverpool (to mark the tenth anniversary of the ex-Beatle's death). The tour sold out in Britain, and gave Kylie some amazing reviews. Next came dates around Asia, ending in Bangkok in May. It was here at the end-of-tour party that Kylie also celebrated her 22nd birthday, with a huge diamond-encrusted ring that Michael had given her during the celebrations. It was also the first time since catching up with each other in Hong Kong that they had seen each other in a month. Perhaps, too, at that point, she must have been feeling that the relationship was one to stay.

In fact, the end of the tour had perfectly coincided with Kylie filming an advert for Coca-Cola, with the release of the new track, 'Better The Devil You Know' … and with friction at PWL. While the single, and in particular the video to accompany it, introduced Kylie's new found confidence in performing and in her image in a big way, Pete Waterman had serious reservations about Kylie's new look. As far as he was concerned it was simply light years away from the image that his label wanted to project for her. The video featured a revealingly dressed, perfectly body-toned Kylie dancing madly, like a wild beast and snuggling herself up into the arms of a naked black man twice her size. But Waterman's bank balance after the huge success of the single put his mind at rest. Kylie's transformation would work, and better than anyone had expected.

Kylie was now thinking more for herself rather than just what pleased others. This was evident from interviews at the time. Quite significantly, she had begun to expand beyond her career and private life, and was touching on more political issues, especially the environment: the recycling of glass and paper, damage to the ozone layer by aerosol sprays, and pollution caused by plastic manufacture. All were exercising her mind and she wanted her public to exercise them as well.

And on another level, since 'Better The Devil You Know' she was seeking more control over her image on a more permanent basis. The innocent girl-next-door vision that PWL had hoped to prolong indefinitely was the one thing that she no longer had any interest in. If anything, she was most probably feeling that they'd had their way for long enough. Perhaps it was Michael's influence that encouraged her to go in with all guns blazing to demand her own wishes. According to some, she almost had to threaten to call it a day before anyone would listen and she could ultimately succeed in her general refusal to compromise her goals. Certainly she wanted to have final approval over all her photo-shoots and video work and, eventually, the same control over the songs she recorded.

Despite all the objections, the so-called controversial video for 'Better The Devil You Know' couldn't have been better received than it was around the club scene. And that pleased Kylie more than anything. Probably for the first time in her career, Kylie was gathering some serious street cred; she was expanding her horizons beyond the teen market that Stock Aitken and Waterman had cornered to a new adult audience, and her public loved it.

The single crashed into the charts at Number Five before peaking – as most of her previous singles had done – at Number Two. It was obvious from that alone that Kylie's choices and determination to change had indeed been the correct ones.

Kylie and Michael would spend much of the next few months flitting between their pads in Hong Kong and Sydney, but come September Michael had to return to London with INXS for the release of *X* and the start of the accompanying international tour. Now it was a matter of getting as much time together as their schedules would allow. Kylie, too, had a new album to promote. *Rhythm of Love* included several numbers from her Los Angeles recording venture in the spring. It would almost be Christmas before they could spend any quality time together again – and for the first time ever Kylie chose to be away from her family over the festive season.

All the same, they had the summer to themselves. They headed off to Europe to spend two weeks in Italy. The South of France was also on the itinerary for the homeward journey where the couple, who were now considered impulsive, bought themselves a four-bedroom villa for just under half a million dollars.

In fact it was while the happy pair were away on foreign turf that the tabloid press would be at it once again, publishing a sneak preview of a spoof art exhibition that had been mounted in a Melbourne gallery during the summer for which a group of Australian artists had been asked to depict Kylie in the style of their favourite painters. The results included a Picasso-style abstract, a Renaissance Madonna complete with baby, and a nude send-up of Chloe, the famous Australian oil painting.

Kylie had never had a problem with nudity, often putting this down to being an Australian. That same summer she commissioned photographer Grant Matthews to take a series of pictures, and among the collection were several nude shots. Even if she was pictured in the usual tasteful way that most of her naked poses are done, the tabloids would certainly have been fighting to get their hands on them, although Kylie would make sure that they never would.

Access to the pictures would be strictly limited, she said at the time, and they would never be seen outside her own immediate circle. Besides Grant Matthews was a trusted friend, and he did not let her down. Not even when *Playboy* magazine were rumoured to have offered half a million pounds for the shots, he would simply refuse to part with them.

Overall, 1990 had proved a good year for Kylie. But there was a sting in the tail by the end. No matter how happy Kylie said she was, speculation was mounting about the cracks show-ing in her relationship with Michael. It was perhaps not that surprising if his sexual reputation was to be believed. With rumours of blistering rows and blissful reconciliations and the couple themselves steering clear of press curiosity, it was left to sister Dannii to assure journalists that the romance was still going strong, even if it wasn't.

# SEVEN

# SHOCKED BY THE POWER

So although the previous twelve months had been wonderful for Kylie, the next few months would prove far more difficult. Her life with Michael Hutchence was ending. Less than two months into the New Year, and having spent their Christmas vacation together, the fairy-tale romance would finally be killed off.

Michael was in the midst of his American stadium tour with INXS to help promote their latest album *X* and with Kylie already into rehearsals for her own Rhythm of Love tour, due to open in Perth in mid-February, many believe that Kylie and Michael only saw each other again at her Sydney show later that same month under strained conditions.

It was there, apparently, that the relationship broke down: Kylie had heard that Michael had been fooling around while on the road and confronted him with the rumours. He didn't even try to deny that he'd been taking in girls at almost every city.

But according to Hutchence biographer, Victor Lovegrove, the end of their relationship was more complicated than that. 'It was one of those situations where you're not sure why you broke up, but you did,' Kylie now remembers.

Apparently it was while Kylie was in Australia preparing for her then forthcoming tour that Michael called her from New York. 'We broke up on the phone,' she told the author. 'I flew to Manhattan so we could talk. He was very strange at that point, and I remember him being somewhere that I'd never seen him before. He was just very distressed. I don't know what he'd been taking or what he'd really been going through, but he was not together.'

Unfortunately it turned out he'd been seeing supermodel Helena Christensen for months.

Michael Hutchence died alone in a Sydney hotel room in late 1997. It appeared that his self-indulgence had finally killed him. The coroner's verdict was that he had committed suicide but there was much speculation that he died carrrying out a bizarre sexual act on himself. During the final years of his life, the couple had begun to patch up their past, and it wasn't until after his death that Kylie found herself fully able to reconcile her continued love for him.

But Kylie to this day appears to remain confused as to why they split. 'He was my first great love and it caused great heartbreak when we split up. I think he eventually wondered why it happened. We had a good thing and I'm sure he never ever wanted to hurt me.

'Maybe he indulged himself in too many projects, whether it be seducing women or reading poetry, taking drugs or staying in the most exquisite hotels. He was the first person I had been extremely close to who has died. But I'm sure he's laughing, looking down now, knowing that he's still teaching me.

opposite:
Kylie and Jason Donovan performed their Number One duet *Especially For You* at the Children's Royal Variety Performance in London, 1989.
© All Action

right:
Outside PWL's studios in London during the recording session of *Do They Know It's Christmas?* Kylie is pictured here with Jason Donovan and Bros in December 1989.
© G Dalla at Camera Press

below:
Always an enjoyment to meet members of the Royal Family, Kylie is shown here meeting the Queen Mother at the Royal Variety Performance in November 1988.
© Duncan Raban at Camera Press

Another early publicity
shot from 1988.
© All Action

Kylie is shown here attending
one of the many music
industry functions she was
invited to during 1988.
© Rex

Not for the first time in her career, Kylie dyed her hair red for a screen role. Here it was for her 1995 movie *Bio-Dome*.
© Richard Young at Rex

Kylie during an album signing session for *Impossible Princess*, London 1998.
© Brian Rasic at Rex

Kylie was again headline news for
the outfit she wore at the MTV Europe
music awards in November 2000.
© Ray Tang at Rex

Kylie is seen here performing *Can't
Get You Out of My Head* at the
San Remo Festival in March 2002.
© Theodore Wood at Camera Press

Kylie with Nick Cave in 1995 at T in the Park.
© Justin Thomas at All Action

Kylie with Robbie Williams performing their hit duet *Kids* at the MTV Europe music awards, November 2000.
© Brian Rasic at Rex

Kylie with her first *real* love, the late Michael Hutchence, in 1990.
© Pat Lyttle at Camera Press

Kylie and James Gooding met at a party in Los Angeles in 1999 and have been together ever since.
© Stewart Mark at Camera Press

Kylie at the *Smash Hits* Poll Winners Party, 2001.
© Brian Rasic at Rex

opposite:
Kylie was watched by over four billion people at the closing ceremony of the
Sydney Olympics 2000 where she performed her own version of Abba's *Dancing Queen*.
© Music Press Pictures

opposite:
Kylie, the Impossible Princess, 1998.
© Music Press Pictures

left:
Kylie at the Rankin Exhibition,
London 1996, with the nude
picture of herself that featured
in the photographer's exhibition.
© William Conran at Camera Press

below:
Kylie with the late Gianni Versace.
© Theodore Wood at Camera Press

Kylie performing *Can't Get You Out of My Head* at the
MTV Europe music awards, November 2000.
© All Action

opposite:
Kylie was crowned 'Queen of the Brits' in February 2002, where she
won two of the four awards she was nominated for, and gave her
most memorable performance of *Can't Get You Out of My Head*.
© Camera Press

Kylie during a special club appearance in Ibiza, 2000, in gold hot pants,
similar to those she made so famous from her *Spinning Around* video.

'Time does heal, but in its own time. Michael's death was so powerful, and yet I miss him as much as a year ago', she said in late 1998. 'Perhaps more. I think of him all the time. I still feel him watching over me very strongly sometimes. It's far more important than I can say.'

And certainly, before he died, Hutchence spoke to his father about Kylie and said that he regretted the way he had treated her.

It was a devastating time for Kylie, but within a few months she would soon be publicly involved with another person – just as Hutchence was with Christiansen – and be on the road to recovery.

Although, following the end of her Rhythm of Love tour in Japan, she had fled to Paris to heal her wounds with a very dear girlfriend for support, the end of the romance with Hutchence had left her emotionally in pieces. It had, nevertheless, made her realise just how important friends are. Certainly, like most people going through break-ups, 'I wouldn't be where I am now without their support.'

Still devastated when the media was forever on her back for some kind of comment, they now wanted to know what she thought of sister Dannii's assault on the British pop scene. But what, after all, could she say? Yes, she had appeared in Kylie's video for 'What Do I Have To Do?' Yes, she had released a single called 'Love and Kisses'.

Kylie could say little to discourage the tittle-tattle of the press, but attempted to prove that she was close to her sister by writing the song 'Love Traffic' for her younger sibling's debut album. The press were unconvinced, one journalist commenting that Kylie had only done so to get one over on Dannii by helping herself to a percentage of her album royalties.

By 1991 Dannii was also a familiar face to British television audiences – as punk girl Emma – in the Australian soap *Home and Away* which was being aired opposite the BBC's lunch and tea-time slots for *Neighbours*. But as for the so-called sibling rivalry between the two, that was just something conjured up by the tabloid press. And both reinforced that whenever they talked with journalists probing that same suggestion.

While it was obvious that Kylie was deeply sad about the outcome of her passionate affair with Hutchence, she had also emerged as a much wiser and more confident person. True, Michael may have broken her heart, but he also changed the way she now regarded herself.

Being with him had unearthed a darker side to her personality – she had discovered the true power of sex and outgrown once and for all her bubbly teenage, girl-next-door persona. It was not simply a matter of wearing black satin instead of fluffy jumpers. Michael had provided her with a potentially far more valuable gift, that of self-awareness and of having the courage of her own convictions. Years later after his traumatic death she continued to remember him with affection and gratitude, neatly fielding the charge that he had corrupted her.

'There wasn't a day when I woke up and thought, whoopee, I've discovered my sexuality,' she reflected in one interview. 'But going out with Michael I realised I was at ease with men, and that I was attractive to them.' At the same though, she also insisted that he had brought far more into her relatively adolescent life than raw sex and the liberating effect of living the high life.

'I was only 21 when we met, and very naive. I learned so much from him – the sex was a small part of a much bigger picture. He helped me to appreciate travel, art, ideas. Above all, he supported me and never tried to make me into something I'm not – and that helped me believe in myself.'

That new level of strength also helped her to face up to media jokes that were doing the rounds at the time. Within months of her break-up, she quickly became the subject of a merciless *Spitting Image* sketch that teamed her latex image alongside those of Rolling Stones Mick Jagger and Bill Wyman. And a month or two after that, satirical magazine *Viz* ran a spoof in which she was holidaying in a caravan in Filey, and was caught sunbathing topless on the windswept North Yorkshire beach. Even if it had made her laugh, tourist chiefs in the northern resort were simply delighted for the exposure.

Kylie was never destined for the solitary life. When she and Hutchence finally went their separate ways, rumours were soon in circulation of a new romance with rock star Lenny Kravitz, but it was South African native Zane O'Donnell who would now be the new man in her life. O'Donnell had been waiting for an opportunity to pursue a relationship with Kylie ever since he had first clapped eyes on her in London late in 1990, playing Kylie's love interest in her 'What Do I Have to Do?' video. He would also go on to feature in the video for 'Shocked' and would appear on the front sleeve for the album *Let's Get To It*.

The gossip columnists, of course, were far more interested in Zane's romantic past. His marriage, for instance, was already in trouble, even then. With wife and son left behind in South Africa when he came to London to pursue an already flourishing career, he had, according to the rumour mill, apparently left his live-in girlfriend, model Daria Lingenberg, to be with Kylie.

It was around this time that his ex-wife Lauren issued a warning about his inability to resist beautiful women. Not that it bothered Kylie. Why should it? She had already decided that the former Levi jeans model was certainly worth taking the risk for.

This was obvious from when she had returned to London after completing the Rhythm of Love tour to immerse herself in the city nightlife, again with Zane constantly by her side. 'You know, that period made me feel part of London,' recalled Kylie. 'It made me feel part of a scene, and if I hear a song from that period it takes me straight back.'

Certainly she had a high profile at the London premiere of *The Commitments*, Alan Parker's critically applauded movie about the rise and fall of a Dublin soul band, and at the opening of the controversial *In Bed with Madonna*, which of course, immediately evoked media comparisons between the two.

One newspaper even consulted a psychologist for an opinion on why Madonna exuded sex appeal and Kylie apparently didn't. The reason put forward was that Madonna's was 'from her soul', while Kylie, on the other hand, still remained for many people, the girl next door, and her new sex image was nothing more than a masquerade.

The comparisons to Madonna would rise to a crescendo during her Let's Get To It tour, but Kylie was by this stage becoming tired of them. 'At first I was flattered to be compared to Madonna' she commented, 'but now I don't want to be second to anybody, and I don't think I am. And image-wise, what hasn't Madonna done?'

But the 'SexKylie' image was taking hold. As if to demonstrate this, even security officers at Heathrow Airport were shocked when they found a pair of handcuffs in the luggage that she was carrying on to a flight. Although the cuffs – items considered capable of being used to restrain a pilot – were returned to her at the end of the flight, the whole thing left Kylie somewhat embarrassed.

'That story will follow me around forever', says Kylie today. 'Everyone looks at me so unconvinced when I explain this. I had this little leather pouch with handcuffs as the handle. I was travelling to Monte Carlo from Heathrow, so I put this small handbag into a larger carrier bag. It never crossed my mind that it would be construed as a dangerous item. I put the bag through the X-ray machine and they took them off me. I believe I still have the bag in a drawer somewhere. That one won't be going to Oxfam. I don't quite know what to do with it.'

Meanwhile interest in her was waning in the US, a far cry from her situation today. Nor did it improve when in August 1991 MCA, who had previously dropped plans to release 'Better The Devil You Know', featured on the soundtrack of a new US movie, turned down the release of her *Rhythm of Love* album in the States. As if to prove that when it rains it pours, they also refused point blank to release 'Shocked', deeming the video that accompanied it, with its sexual undertones, as unsuitable for the American market. Needless to say, elsewhere in the world the single became yet another international hit.

Not to be discouraged, a little over two months later in October 1991, Kylie was back in London for the British Fashion Awards with an elegant gold lamé outfit that immediately elicited comparisons with 1960s screen legend Brigitte Bardot. She also appeared on the cover of *The Face* in which she was dubbed 'the new cultural icon' by its editor. A little after that, *NME* called her the 'Goddess of Pop'. As if that wasn't enough to convince anyone, she was named 'Date of the Month' in *Esquire* and even won herself a lavish fashion spread in *Vogue* magazine.

That same month Kylie embarked on her final tour for the foreseeable future through the UK and Europe. The Let's Get To

It tour was an updated version of the Australian version of the Rhythm Of Love tour from earlier in the year. Part of that *update* was a whole new stage wardrobe, the very thing that caused uproar. The reviews for her new raunchy shows included bitter criticism for Kylie's choice of costume.

Showing remarkable taste and foresight, she collaborated on her wardrobe with John Galliano, now one of the world's pre-eminent fashion designers. However, to some of her more traditional fans it may have seemed like a case of 'the Empress's New Clothes', given that she often wore little other than raunchy underwear – G-strings, bras, suspenders and fishnets. Other tricks included peeling off one of Galliano's tight black evening dresses to reveal small and very tight black shorts; singing 'I Should Be So Lucky' dressed as a bizarre cross between a dominatrix and a bus conductor, black vinyl corsets and at other times, very little else. It was, protested some parents who had taken their youngsters expecting to see a post-*Neighbours* Kylie, a long way from the little suit and baggy cap she had worn on her first tour. As far as the media were concerned, it simply enforced their opinion that Kylie was merely trying to copy Madonna – 'Who's That Girl?' screamed one tabloid cover the morning after the first show, depicting a close-up of Kylie's body-stocking-covered buttocks. From there the comparisons went into overdrive.

Kylie had indeed used Madonna's old producer and song-writer on the *Rhythm of Love* album, but the tabloids failed to mention she had also used those who had worked with other female singers such as Martika and Paula Abdul. Perhaps she had also seemingly made the mistake of mentioning Madonna as being one of her influences some years earlier.

At the same time as her tour, Kylie released her final studio album for PWL. Things had changed there too. Matt Aitken had left the company early in 1991 to pursue his first real love and interest in motor racing. Kylie requested she co-write half the songs on the album with Aitken's previous writing partner Mike Stock. Not that it would prove an easy task. At least at the outset Stock felt that she was writing purely for the sake of it, and there was no real point. Whether this was true or not, *Let's Get To It* became the first of her albums to have a personal feel, with influences from her own tastes in music.

In the end, Kylie considered that the R&B approach she had used to make up the tracks for *Let's Get To It*, with her new compositions with Stock, would end up being her favourite over and above all the other recordings she had done up to that point in her career.

The credible music press agreed with her, labelling the album a 'masterpiece' and crowning Kylie a 'genius of pop'. The first single considered for release was the ballad 'Finer Feelings', containing lyrics which referred to 'Sexual Healing' by Marvin Gaye, one of her favourite songs. But the track was ultimately put on hold to make way for the 'jazz band pop' of 'Word Is Out' which was considered safer. But maybe those making such decisions at her record label had possibly made an incorrect choice. Had the departure of Matt Aitken and the restructuring of PWL, including a buyout by the multinational Time Warner, caused a greater dent than had been thought?

It was the first time one of her singles had not entered the Top Ten in the UK and its failure to reach the heights of previous singles was largely put down to the video, which featured Kylie, in stockings and suspenders on the streets, and her accompanying TV promotion which followed the same theme. 'The public saw Kylie dressed as a prostitute', Pete Waterman recalls. 'And they wouldn't accept it.'

In some quarters it also pointed towards yet another change in musical direction, although minor compared to what was to come. Perhaps that was the reason for the seeming lack of interest in the release. Kylie's Australian label thought so, and instead decided upon releasing a radically remixed, and much improved, version of the song, minus the synthesised band sound.

By now, of course, Kylie was being hailed as the one-hit wonder that she had been greeted as at the start of her career, even though she clearly wasn't. It probably didn't help either that she hadn't taken on any promotional activity in recent years. And perhaps, if there was any one thing that she should have done, it would have been to maintain her once high-profile public life.

In an attempt to revitalise her career, the song 'If You Were With Me Now', a duet with little known US soul singer Keith Washington, was released towards the end of the year. It was a romantic ballad, free of sexual references and to accompany it was a similarly sex-free, gloriously glamorous video in which Kylie was seen in a dozen outfits. Once again, the track took Kylie back in the Top Five and everyone sighed with relief.

Although she would spend much of 1992 away from the spotlight, perhaps it was not that surprising. She had, after all, lived half her life in the goldfish bowl of celebrity and the pressure had finally taken its toll on her. She did, of course, do the promotional work for each release for which she was contracted, but nothing more.

She needed time to take stock: her life had ceased to be mundane once *Neighbours* had taken off and, with it, the growth of her fame. Perhaps too, her elaborate dream to retreat from the hype of it all, by going to university or backpacking around

Europe or even a long-distance road trip was becoming a thing of the past. Seventeen hit records in little more than four years had resulted in three and a half of those years under constant exposure to the demands of being a teen star, and in that time, she had suffered nervous exhaustion on several occasions, plus many more minor illnesses.

In addition to that, of course, she had the stress of her failed relationship with Michael Hutchence, an increasingly hostile press, and with two of her last four singles failing to make the Top Ten, no wonder she longed to get away from it all for a while.

And who could blame her? In fact, it was soon after the release of her 18th single, 'Finer Feelings', in April 1992 that she decided she would see out much of the rest of the year enjoying a life free from work commitments. 'The clichés about the price of fame are true. I push myself to the limit, and then I collapse. The day after a tour I fall ill.'

All the same she would return to her public life every now and then. She agreed to take part in 'Trading Places' – a high-profile fundraising event which would in the end contribute towards the £15 million needed to set up the world's first breast cancer research centre. It was an event where fans were invited to seek sponsorship for the pleasure of becoming their favourite star for a day.

'I hope you enjoy being me as much as I do,' Kylie wrote in the booklet she provided to enable those taking part to come as close as possible to her real self. Her tips covered everything from changing hairstyles at least three times a day, dancing their lycra leggings off, and appointing a friend to play the part of Yvonne, her trusted personal assistant, who also doubled as hairdresser to take care of the necessary style changes.

Zane O'Donnell was still very much in the picture and although the couple were together in Paris for several months, living in a friend's apartment and keeping their media exposure very much in check, they never allowed matters to snowball out of control. She was still avoiding all the attendant touring and publicity duties that filled so much of her time in previous years, but for the moment, at any rate, she was quite happy to enjoy the freedom of being in between projects.

Her absence from public life also gave rise to rumour upon rumour. Even when she did reappear in the spotlight, perhaps she became equally sick of having to answer the countless questions that were thrown at her. Where had she been? What did she have to hide?

Among the myriad of disasters that the press attributed to her absence, plastic surgery was at the top of the list. Now on top of everything else, she would also have to defend herself against those who openly accused her of having a boob job and collagen implants to plump out her pout.

She also made another life-enhancing decision, and that was to set up a permanent base in London. Although she still kept her properties in Australia, one of which served exclusively as her own retreat, she decided upon a sixth-floor apartment in West London.

Still under contract to PWL, the label would release four singles over the year. Only one, 'Give Me Just A Little More Time', came close to the success of her previous hits by going to Number Two and staying in the chart for another eight weeks. The other three, 'Finer Feelings', 'What Kind Of Fool' and 'Celebration', only made the Top Twenty. Even so, it was hard to ignore the fact that Kylie's fifteen minutes of fame had already stretched to five years, and now with her new iconic status was set to last even longer.

Kylie's contract with PWL was due to expire at the end of 1992, exactly five years after she had signed on the dotted line for the release of 'I Should Be So Lucky', and with little more than that one song in mind. No-one could have believed then that she would see out the full term of the contract, and with such success. To round off her time at the Hit Factory, and as part of the contract, PWL released her final album on the label. *Kylie's Greatest Hits* and its accompanying *Greatest Video Hits* was an amazing document of five very busy years in the music business, and all the highlights of her career to date including five Number Ones. And quite appropriately, the collection placed Kylie back on top of the British charts once again.

Kylie appeared at the *Smash Hits* awards at London's Olympia in December, alongside new boy band Take That. She performed 'Celebration' – the 1980s classic from Kool And The Gang – often quoted as being her 'favourite song of all time' during her years at PWL, and of course, her final single for the label.

Resplendent in a white, slash-fronted Elvis outfit, and surrounded by most of the dancers she had used over the previous five years, the performance was poignant. This was her 'farewell' appearance, her last for PWL, and nobody knew what Chameleon Kylie would come back with next, or indeed whether she would be back at all.

# EIGHT

# DECONSTRUCTING KYLIE

Following Christmas 1992, Kylie was about to start a new phase in her remarkable music career. The production process for churning out hit after hit favoured by the PWL label was by now losing much of its original appeal for Kylie who no longer wanted to be marketed as yet another slice of typical pop merchandise, even though that was the way Peter Waterman and Mike Stock had previously garnered much of their success.

But the magical elixir from the PWL stable was now becoming more and more elusive. Although they were still putting out records at the same rate as before, they weren't all necessarily becoming hits. And if Kylie was to survive musically as an artist then she needed to discover new ways to gain artistic credibility and prove, once and for all, that she was more than a commercial lightweight, and not just another passing product of manufactured pop.

By the end of 1992, Kylie's contract with PWL had come to a satisfactory end. And with it, the relationship that catapulted her to pop stardom was finally laid to rest. But she had her concerns. 'I didn't really know what I was doing when I left PWL,' she now says.

Despite her fears, however, in the run up to the end of her contract, PWL had possibly set her free in a way she didn't think was even possible. Her final studio album *Let's Get To It* may have been regarded as commercially unsuccessful compared with previous releases, but the album had nevertheless scored an unexpected critical triumph.

After dismissing Kylie as trite, talentless froth for more than three years, the more sophisticated music papers such as *NME* and *Melody Maker* had undergone a change of heart. They were so bowled over by the spirit of her rhythm and blues album that they hailed her as an exceptional pop talent.

Both album and Kylie had also caught the attention of another musical genius – the enigmatic artist then still known as Prince. She had admired and worshipped him and his music for as long as she could remember. Even at the height her fame, almost four years earlier and then still very much the girl-next-door, Kylie, like so many other teenagers before her, would prob-ably place meeting her idol above all else.

Little did she know then that in little more than three years she would have that opportunity. Even more amazing was how simply it all came about. Prince had hired the same security crew for his late 1992 UK tour as Kylie had the previous year, so one can only imagine the excitement she must have felt when Prince finally invited her backstage to meet him.

From that initial introduction, she was invited to Paisley Park, the singer's secret hideaway in Minneapolis – one of the

Midwest's most beautiful cities – during another visit she made only days later, under his request, to visit him at his London recording studio.

When finally taking up his invitation, which of course she jumped at, it she turned up with the lyrics of a song she had written provisionally titled 'Baby Doll', hoping that he'd put some music to her words – and he did.

Their friendship also triggered off a whole wave of press speculation, especially since Kylie had once referred to the diminutive star as the only artist that she considered outrageous as much as he was different. Even though he may have revolted some people, others described him as nothing less than sex on legs. Perhaps she did too, but, of course, she denied that there was anything more to it than a genuine interest in the music he was creating.

Speculation about the nature of their relationship might have been less if she hadn't spent so much time with him. 'I hung out there for a while and got to know something of Prince and he is a really reserved character. What I got to know about him, I liked and he's fun. He's a little weird but I'd be disappointed if he wasn't.'

But as for anything romantic, that was simply out of the question. As Kylie herself would later explain, 'I think he's always a bit on the fresh side. But who wants to be on that list? I wonder how many other girls have been lured to Minneapolis? If that's what he enjoys fine, but I'm interested in his music, nothing else.' And although she reinforced that and also hoped that he may have had some interest in what she was also doing in the studio, she remained firmly adamant that she would prefer just to wait and see what the future would hold.

It was in April 1993 that her recording career in particular was about to take a turn in a direction she hadn't expected. After a few months of being without a new record deal since leaving PWL, it seemed the positive reaction of the significant music press coverage for her album was about to pay off. Probably against all of her expectations, she soon found that there were a number of major record labels, like EMI and A&M among others, interested in signing her up, although she was in no hurry to make any decision quite yet.

Taking one step at a time, and as pleased as she must have been with such offers, she was also acutely aware that she didn't want to fall back into the same market catered for by PWL, which she had just left. If anything she wanted to establish lasting credibility for herself.

It seemed that Pete Hatfield and Keith Blackhurst, then cohorts in the highly successful dance music label, deConstruction, had spotted something in Kylie that no one had previously, Hatfield commenting that he saw Kylie as 'a potential radical dance diva'. She, too, was thinking along those same lines.

'I think she felt uncertain about her position in the pop world', comments Hatfield today. 'Certainly she wasn't regarded as the icon she is now. I think there was an idea that she wanted to join something cooler and make a cooler record.'

'I did meet with lots of record companies,' remembers Kylie. 'I liked deConstruction's attitude, I quite liked their arrogance, and I liked the vision they had. It was all very new and exciting. There wouldn't be much point in leaving PWL and going somewhere exactly the same, so it was a big change.'

It was in April 1993 that Kylie signed up with the label in a deal that above all else would offer her the chance to have unique freedom in her decisions, both musically and artistically. That in itself was quite an unusual step for a record company to relinquish.

All the same the small independent subsidiary of BMG-UK and its affiliated parent company RCA Records knew what they were doing. They had already earned themselves a solid reputation for acquiring quality artists with rare talent, many of whom would go on to scoop top awards.

Steve Anderson, along with partner Dave Seaman, as production and remixing team Brothers In Rhythm, was brought in to work closely with Kylie on material for the album. They had collaborated previously on remixing Kylie's single 'Finer Feelings', released in 1992, which Anderson considers 'one of the best songs SAW ever wrote for her'.

The collaboration had worked extremely well and the single was cited as one of Kylie's strongest and most credible for PWL, and both members of Brothers In Rhythm were extremely keen to rekindle the relationship with Kylie.

'I first met Kylie just after deConstruction signed her, and we virtually begged them to consider us to work with her,' Anderson remembers. 'She came out to our studio and had a meeting which set up the original sessions.'

Kylie's relationship with Steve Anderson continues to this day not only as her closest and most regular musical collaboration but as a strong mutual friendship. 'Kylie is the most professional person I have ever worked with,' says Anderson, 'and I count her as a close friend.'

In September 1994 her first single for the label, 'Confide in Me', was released. It was her first since 'Celebration' had come out in November 1992, and with a 32-piece orchestral backing and some remarkable mellifluous vocals by Kylie, it seemed the perfect choice to launch her debut with the new label.

With many considering the recording to be her most sophisticated to date with an unusually sparse arrangement and exotic mood, the single entered the UK chart at Number Two, only just pipped by Whigfield's 'Saturday Night', even though Kylie sold more than enough to place her in the pinnacle position. At home in Australia, of course, perhaps not surprisingly, that is exactly what it did.

One month later, *Kylie Minogue*, her first studio album for three years followed. If credibility was the agenda at work here, then it certainly worked. The songwriting and production credits alone would ensure that. The cream of some of the most influential dance and pop names were represented: Brothers In Rhythm, Farley and Heller, Jimmy Harry, Pet Shop Boys and M People.

Saint Etienne and Rapino Brothers also worked on some excellent tracks, but these were not used in the final. Many others were quoted in the British music press as being desperate to contribute, others stating that they had been approached but were, devastatingly it would seem, too busy with other projects to be involved. At one stage it appeared that every credible production or writing team in the country had a hand in the album.

'I was very flattered to know that a whole lot of people wanted to work on the album and had suggestions for it,' said Kylie shortly after. 'Sometimes I feel like I have a lucky star or something, because, I don't know, why me? How come I'm so fortunate?

'The mere fact that so many people, and especially deConstruction, could see through what I'd done before and know there was more. I suppose it's just a change from years ago, having people not believe in me at all. If you have someone's belief in you, you can do anything. That's one thing I've learned.'

Although Kylie herself was missing from all but one of the songwriting credits; she had actually written eight tracks with Rapino Brothers, who had also produced them, at the beginning of the work for the album in 1993.

Some tracks were excellent, but as a whole the work was deemed to be taking Kylie in the wrong direction and all the tracks that had been laid down were ultimately scrapped. Only one, 'Automatic Love', was given over to Brothers In Rhythm, eventually the main producers for the album, to update in their own style.

In fact, ironically, given the amount of songwriting talent she had to collaborate with, three of the songs on the final album are cover versions: 'Where Is The Feeling?', 'Time Will Pass You By' and 'Where Has The Love Gone?', all of which are rarely known tracks poached by the A&R team at deConstruction.

Indeed, the collection of upbeat dance tracks, lightweight funky numbers and smoochy ballads was received with enthusiasm and appreciation by the reputable music press. One reviewer called her a soul diva. Another claimed it stretched her to the outer limits of her emotional and musical range.

Even the cover illustrated that chameleon quality by presenting a completely new image. Gone was the girl next-door, the pouting sex kitten, the X-certificate raunch. The new Kylie was demure and restrained, in a decorous suit and Miss Moneypenny specs – with just a hint of the mystery and potential beloved of the 'My God, Miss Jones, you're beautiful' school of old movies.

The album was accompanied by the release of some new photographs portraying Kylie's scantily-clad figure in a variety of seductive poses: on hands and knees in skimpy T-shirt and knickers; wanton in hot pants and laddered tights and as seductive as ever in see-through bikini bottom and top. At the time, of course, it did nothing more than garner further allegations that she was trying to duplicate what Madonna had done a few years earlier.

Nor was the criticism helped by the simultaneous publication of a limited-edition coffee-table book that featured even more pictures of Kylie in more or less the same kind of pose. The tabloid press branded it as reminiscent of Madonna's highly controversial *Sex* book, again from a few years earlier. But that, Kylie swore, 'would be incredibly foolish of me'.

'I had plans to do a book before *Sex* came out, not with soft porn pictures though – just a coffee-table book with really nice images in it,' said Kylie, who had worked alongside photographer friend and long-time collaborator Ellen Von Unwerth for the book. 'Are they steamy? Yes. I had to suggest I wear more clothes, but those are the sort of pictures Ellen takes.'

The tabloids failed to mention that Kylie's book was never commercially available, but a limited edition sent out to high-flyers in the fashion, art and music worlds to promote the launch of her new album. Despite this Kylie found herself constantly having to defend her decision to publish the book, even if it was beautifully put together.

Kylie admitted that a set of nude pictures had also been taken at the same time, but she vowed that she would never allow them to be published – not at least for another twenty years or so. One would surface in a more lavish book put together by Kylie in 1999, but it was a very discreet shot taken from some distance.

In the same month as the book came out, and not for the first time in her career, Kylie did, in fact, appear nude on the cover of *Sky* magazine. Picture editor Kay Webb's brief to photographer Neil Davenport – hand-picked so that Kylie would feel comfortable stripping off – was a fresh and natural look, sexy but not vulgar.

In the end, he posed her with arms crossed and legs carefully arranged to ensure readers would see nothing. With hair hanging casually down to her bare shoulders, and with a demure expression on her face, she appeared almost like Patsy Kensit or at least that's how it was then described. She looked much the same as she did years later when she appeared on the front cover of *The Face*, again naked except for red and white striped knickers and brown leather cowboy boots.

The photo-shoot for *Sky* had taken place in Los Angeles. As usual, she insisted on a closed set and took total creative control, retaining copyright of the pictures. She was only too aware that such controversial shots would be in demand and she wanted to make sure she had safeguarded herself against their use anywhere else which did not meet with her approval. Perhaps she was also feeling somewhat troubled over the fact that her new deConstruction album would not be getting a wide release in the States, rather in the same way as for her final two studio albums for PWL.

Even though she had a new label in the USA, being released on the Imago Records label, her latest work would never see the light of day there. 'Confide In Me', having reached high in the US Dance Chart, did see a commercial release, but within days of it hitting stores Imago were facing internal problems and quickly withdrew all current releases. But although her bad luck in the US continued, she didn't need to worry – the situation had to change sooner or later.

And change it finally did, even though it would be as late as February 2002 when, now signed to EMI's American counterpart Capitol, she released 'Can't Get You Out Of My Head' to rave reviews, massive radio air-play and a promotional campaign to make sure this time that the territory was conquered, which was evident from the yells, screams and shouts that greeted her on the *Jay Leno Show* and later during an album signing at the Virgin Megastore in Times Square.

Back in 1993, her career was all set for another flowering. And that alone gave her an entrée to places denied to mere ordinary mortals. In the summer she had again met Prince Charles at a polo match and after a brief security hiccup, she received a warm welcome at a £30,000 after-show bash thrown at Wembley Arena by the latest boy band craze, Take That.

According to one tabloid report, Robbie Williams, then a callow 19-year-old, was left trembling with delight when Kylie gave him a hug and a kiss on the cheek. As for so many others, 'she's my number one dream girl,' he confessed. 'She's gorgeous and frail. You feel like you want to protect her.'

By July 1993, Jason Donovan, who had fallen foul of the gay lobby in the wake of his courtroom run-in with *The Face* magazine, was the party-pooper. Although he had successfully sued the publication in 1991, he had returned most of the £200,000 damages he won when it later emerged that such a huge payout could, indeed, close down the notable monthly publication.

Even though Kylie had supported Jason through much of the case, she was understandably furious when he suddenly decided it was time to go public about the true nature of their past.

After all, wasn't it Jason who had persisted with the constant denials that he and Kylie were in a relationship during the heady Scott and Charlene saga of *Neighbours*? But now with a change of heart, for whatever reason, he was about to reveal all. To both the astonishment and glee of millions of listeners, he told Radio 1 presenter Steve Wright, live on air, that they had not only been a couple for four years, but that they had enjoyed a fully sexual relationship.

The revelation may have shocked Steve Wright, but Kylie was both astounded and furious. And her fury was completely understandable. Even if she didn't offer any explanation to confirm or deny the claims Jason had just hung out in public, perhaps what she couldn't fathom was why he had felt the need to reveal it after all this time? What could possibly be achieved? Although she had never been comfortable with the deception in the first place, she certainly had no interest in going along with Jason's scheme now. Besides, what would have been the point?

She didn't have to seethe for long. In keeping with her new grown-up image, she made a courageous decision – all the more so since it could be regarded as a calculated attempt to shake off any last vestiges of her teenage years and remain both visible and successful, even though she was clearly distancing herself from her past. By choosing to play a live gig, her first for over two years, at the Bang Club, one of London's most established and notorious gay nightclubs, she was in effect re-emerging as loudly as she could.

If her decision may have astounded, or even disappointed her former teen fans, the gay community were absolutely delighted to have their loyalty acknowledged in such a high-profile manner.

The midnight performance, attended by some 2,000 devotees, was the finale to London's Gay Pride Day and was sold out within hours of tickets going on sale, incontrovertible evidence of the way in which Kylie's global gay following had been growing steadily since the early days of her career.

Even back in 1988 drag queens from and around Melbourne had constantly paid tribute to her by staging Kylie revues and sending up her early hits. If those around the then rather naive Kylie of the late Eighties didn't know what to think about such adulation, the gay community was the one area of American society in which Kylie had succeeded in making her mark, for whatever reason. After all, while her albums had never been widely released across the pond, and to most record buyers in the States she remained a one-hit wonder after the release of her cover of Little Eva's original 1962 'Locomotion', to gay men who adorned the nightclubs, she was a huge icon alongside Dusty Springfield, Barbra Streisand and Judy Garland.

'Doing Mardi Gras and Bang was a chance to say thank you. I know the gay community was supporting me when everyone else was slagging me off.'

With the gay fan following that continued to grow in adulation of her, Kylie would again pay further homage to the community with a headlining appearance at yet another major celebration. This time it was in Sydney for the party that followed the annual Gay and Lesbian Mardi Gras parade. 'I felt like I owed it to them because they supported me years before anyone else did.'

She was moved then by the loyalty of the gay community and it is something she has not forgotten since. 'I feel touched to have the opportunity to say thank you.' In the end, that support landed her a vote for the Best Gay Club Act of 1993. It was something that would encourage her to repeat similar appearances time and again, each one with the same raucous reception.

Kylie's appearance was more sedate at her sister's wedding to the ex-Australian Prime Minister's son, Julian McMahon, at the beginning of 1994. She was simply overjoyed to be her bridesmaid. She had always thought Dannii would settle down long before she herself would.

Sadly, the marriage lasted less than twelve months. With the pressure of the career conflicts that kept the couple separated for so much of the time, and both of them often working on opposite sides of the globe, it was no wonder the relationship didn't survive. Although their break-up was said to have been amicable, some insiders suggested there was more going on beneath the surface. Dannii, of course, was saddened by the failure of her married life but later swore it would not deter her from tying the knot again.

Nor did it put Kylie off either. As late as February 2002, she would again repeat her wish for a family of her own. Her father had been an only child, but she wanted at least two children. For the time being though, with Zane O'Donnell now out of her life and with no-one new to take his place either in or out of bed, she probably knew that she was nowhere near to fulfilling that long-held desire.

Indeed, Kylie's revitalised career rapidly awakened new media interest in her private life as well, and during the first six months of 1994, it seemed she only needed to be in the same room or exchange greetings with the opposite sex for the rumour mill to start the tattle about love, romance and even marriage proposals.

One of those occasions was soon after Dannii's wedding when she had met, some say at her own request, Evan Dando, the strapping lead vocalist with top American band the Lemonheads, later linked to actress Winona Ryder.

In fact, it was when the three-piece group was on tour in Australia and Kylie was spotted at two of their gigs in one week that the gossip spread. Staying on for the after-show parties, having nights out in Melbourne, and openly kissing each other at a city club just added fuel to the fire.

But according to Kylie, none of that was true. Although they may have hung out together for a couple of nights, they were not, she insisted, a couple. And neither were any of the dozens of others she was publicly linked to. Although she was close friends with native New Yorker Lenny Kravitz again, they weren't anything more than just good friends. The truth was that Kylie hadn't been involved in a serious relationship since her split with Zane O'Donnell.

Less than a month after that barely worth mentioning 'fling' with Dando, Kylie and Michael Hutchence, now friends again, had a brief reunion of sorts. With his then current girlfriend Helena Christensen away on a modelling assignment in the US, they met during an INXS tour of Australia at an after-show party but no-one actually saw them do anything untoward.

Perhaps the most mystifying rumour of all was that of her dalliance with Julian Lennon the musician son of the late lamented ex-Beatle. In March 1994 one of the more sensational tabloid dailies published an exclusive report of a Los Angeles love-nest. Among the claims were meetings with Julian's mother Cynthia, plans to move clothes and belongings into his hillside home, and even suggestions that wedding bells would soon be ringing. Once again, Kylie couldn't believe such gossip. She had apparently come across Lennon only once – in a nightclub in 1992.

As if that was not enough, according to even more tabloid press coverage, Prince – as he was then still known – and without girlfriend Nona Gaye in tow, had stayed in touch with Kylie ever since her visit to his Minneapolis home, and when they met again a year later, it was surrounded by huge media curiosity with the usual speculation.

They played the game that the rumour mill was hoping for of course. Just weeks away from Kylie's 26th birthday, at the after-show party to celebrate the prestigious annual World Music Awards in Monte Carlo, they were seen slow-dancing cheek to cheek to Prince's own global hit 'The Most Beautiful Girl In The World', watched over by Michael Hutchence, now back with Helena Christensen.

But she would not be letting Prince or anyone else into her romantic life. Besides, she insisted at the time, she had never even snogged him, as she put it – it was simply that as they were of similar height they both enjoyed dancing together without having to look straight into the other's waistline!

In the absence of a serious relationship to fill the gap left by Zane, and with a new album scheduled for that summer, there was also a new movie lined up: her first Hollywood-funded project since *The Delinquents*.

It just so happened that film director Steven de Souza was on the lookout for a British actress to fill the role of Intelligence Officer Cammy in his new screen adaptation of the Nintendo 'Beat-'em-up game' *Street Fighter*. Having spotted Kylie in a magazine, he like many others had become intrigued by the incredible presence she possessed in front of the camera and, having read in the accompanying article that she had originally been an actress, he decided to investigate further.

Not even when he discovered that she was an Australian native was he put off. If anything it intrigued him to sit through some old footage of her previous work. And when he did, barely noticing any trace of an Australian accent, he remembers his search ended then and there. Without an audition or even a screen test he immediately offered Kylie the part as soon as he could. She, of course, accepted.

Her role would involve kick boxing, snapping the necks of the enemy and blasting her way through walls with a bazooka. As

*Sky* magazine coined it, this was 'Kickass Kylie'! And although certainly not Shakespeare, it would still prove to strike a profitable chord with audiences, and would indeed pave the trail for Kylie to establish herself at the US box office.

'I sometimes wonder if I have a lucky star,' Kylie was moved to observe once more after she flew to Thailand to join the cast with no audition or screen test. At the time she wasn't even looking towards movies since promoting her new album and making the video to go with it were top of her priorities. But being head-hunted for a major action blockbuster had a certain appeal, even if it does entail spending a month in Bangkok during the hottest, steamiest, most uncomfortable time of the year.

All the same, she accepted the role without hesitation. And de Souza couldn't have been more delighted. Even though he had considered many other actresses for Kylie's role, every one had lacked the ability to wrap their accents around the plummy vowels of a proper English miss. Neither did they have the physical attraction that Kylie had, or even the ability to appear as intelligent as she did.

Even if Kylie had fallen short of the physical attributes of the character she would be playing, she quickly set about rectifying matters in the best way she knew. For almost the entire 12-week shooting schedule, she was up at the crack of dawn, at 4.30 every morning, for a punishing working-out schedule in the gym to build up stamina, strength and her muscles. 'If only I got gym miles the same as people get air miles,' joked Kylie. 'I'm finding muscles where I didn't know muscles existed.'

But mere physical fitness wasn't enough. Inspirational Kung Fu ace Benny 'The Jet' Uquidz was brought in to provide intensive martial arts training. He too was thoroughly impressed with her commitment.

'She had the rhythm, and she picked it up very quickly,' he enthused. High praise indeed from the man who had taught Chuck Norris combat technique and had devised similar fitness training programmes for the likes of Sylvester Stallone, Michelle Pfeiffer and Keanu Reeves. He had even become the subject of a song by Elton John.

Although still only a featherweight at the end of her training, she certainly appeared well toned and curvier than ever before. As for the suggestion that she had boosted her breasts to 34B, she would simply laugh at the rumour. Far more important was the sense of focus and determination she had been able to tune in with her body. It enabled her to make the most of her small but fragile frame. 'I've learned so much about my body, but I suppose it's sexy to be aware of it instead of letting it slump in a chair all day.'

She proved this in camera stunts, kicking one assailant very precisely in the head and jumping on another's shoulders to snap his neck. She even learned to spray bullets from a Beretta long before Angelina Jolie did much the same for *Lara Croft: Tomb Raider* some years later.

Jean-Claude Van Damme was simply thrilled to be working with her. 'She makes me look bigger,' he smiled during an on-set interview, glancing around at some of the other, more strapping, supporting players. Even with such complimentary comments, Van Damme still left Kylie cold. 'He fancies himself as a ladies man,' she later said. 'I try to be polite, but he has this thing about being the big man on set.'

While *Street Fighter* proved a considerable commercial success, grossing $70 million at the American box office, it did nothing to ensure Kylie a firm place in Hollywood, although she would still return to acting every now and then. Today, however, it is almost impossible to coax Kylie into speaking about *Street*

*Fighter*, or indeed any of the other movies she has made, except for her first, *The Delinquents*, of which she remains very proud.

As *Street Fighter* topped box office charts around the world, a new single, 'Put Yourself In My Place', became the perfect close to 1994, and with it one of Kylie's most talked about videos. It featured a *Barbarella* pastiche with Kylie decked out in a 'hot pink spacesuit' stripping off in the comfort of her own spaceship.

Despite the enjoyment she had in making *Street Fighter*, the lack of personal fulfilment she had gained from the experience as a whole would encourage her to throw herself into her music in a big way. Her 'comeback' was complete: with two new successful singles and an album to her name, deConstruction were now confident in trusting Kylie's intuition.

# NINE

# THE WILD ROSE

By the time Kylie had returned to Australia it was December 1994. And no matter what else, there was one thing that she was determined not to break, and that was celebrating the festive season and New Year in Melbourne. Having not long completed another gruelling round of promotional activity for her then latest single throughout most of Europe in the latter stages of 1994, she was more resolute than ever to spend Christmas at home with her family and to stay over longer than she had in previous years.

It was also ideal for the special celebration gig on New Year's Eve in Sydney she was planning as a thank you and acknowledgement to the gay fan following that had continued to support her through thick and thin. And what an occasion. Singing live to pre-recorded backing tapes for more than 5,000 partygoers, including her entire family, close friends, dancers and a line-up of lookalike drag queens, for the forty minutes she was on stage, her performance was memorable.

Even though she had adopted a spontaneous approach, it was apparent that such spontaneity was her chosen path for playing live gigs. Perhaps the weeks and months of exhausting headlining tours, living out of suitcases and hotel rooms, and being dashed into one stadium after another full of screaming kids, had finally taken its toll on her; it no longer appealed to her.

And with little or no work obligations following the end of December gig, and now no longer concerned about working herself to the point of exhaustion, aware of her own limitations, for the time being all she wanted to do was live a normal life for a while without any outside pressure or stress.

She would spend the first three months of 1995 in Australia enjoying such delights as her mother's home cooking and catching up with more personal things, such as reunions with friends, family and ex-boyfriends, Michael Hutchence and Jason Donovan among others.

Even if she felt a little guilty about this lapse from her usual strict work routine, she could expunge the transgression by following her golden rule to make time available for the things that pleased her most. For 1995, this meant co-hosting a local television show, making a movie or two, and teaming up with a fellow Australian musician who was to become one of the biggest influences on her career. Not that she knew what lay ahead for her, nor cared – she just wanted to enjoy her free time. Not only that but there was also a new romance on the horizon.

That romance – or fling, as it would probably be better described – was with Mark Gerber, the former model turned actor and rock singer who had just come into her life. Some of the star-spotters who first saw the couple together that January observed that he bore an uncanny resemblance to Kylie's ex, Zane O'Donnell.

Gerber had recently landed a starring role in *Sirens*, one of the most successful movies of that year in Australian cinema, for which he had worked alongside such names as Hugh Grant, Sam Neill and another model turned actor, Elle McPherson.

Gerber's role as a blind stable hand had required a certain amount of nude and semi-nude scenes for the almost voyeuristic benefit of the cameras. Needless to say, when he and Kylie went public with their relationship, it was another match made in tabloid heaven. Most assumed she had fallen for what she had seen of his naked body on the screen before she actually fell for him in real life.

But whatever the origins of the romance, that acquaintance, it seemed, would become far more serious during a cruise around Sydney Harbour. According to observers it was from that moment that they became inseparable. The same moment, in fact, that they were literally hounded by paparazzi, desperate to snap anything they could of the new couple, including occasions such as Gerber's gigs with his rock band, Flame Boa, for whom he played bass.

But Gerber's mother didn't seem too happy to see her beloved Mark splashed across the daily tabloids, all because of his relationship with this pop star. The final straw had been Kylie's attendance at an art exhibition held by Gerber's artistic brother. Her presence had overshadowed the whole affair, creating yet more scurrilous media gossip.

It's possible that Mrs Gerber found another woman's affections for her son difficult to cope with, although she need not have worried. According to friends from both quarters, the relationship was already troubled when Kylie's aspirations for Mark far outstripped his own vision for his future. Having told Gerber that rock music and TV commercials just weren't enough for a career, it seems that such demands for him to look out for more promising work had created the conflict that finally broke them up.

The end of Kylie's Australian holiday publicly revealed what the gossip grapevine had been insisting on for weeks – that Kylie and Mark Gerber weren't together any more. But despite speculation to the contrary – that Gerber was left inconsolable at the end of the romance – nothing could have been further from the truth. By the time they had gone their separate ways, it would soon become clear that it was Gerber who had decided to opt out of the paparazzi merry-go-round which surrounded Kylie's private and public life. Perhaps, too, with his ex-girlfriend coming back into his life, he just felt he'd had enough.

Kylie was as philosophical as ever about the way Gerber ended the relationship, or at least she was in public. Even though she believed 'romance is wonderful, my career is so much at the forefront that any relationship has to be secondary'. Indeed, it was then that her priorities for returning to work seemed to change. She was the first to admit that she couldn't spend too long without working before she was itching to get back into the studio or begin writing songs.

She would now take on two of her most unlikely projects. One was a short art-house film entitled *Hayride to Hell*, and the other would be the controversial recording session that she was determined to undertake with Nick Cave.

Cave was the lead vocalist and driving force behind his band, the Bad Seeds, and Melbourne's other international music icon. He had had a cult following for a decade, although he had never known commercial success like Kylie's. Cave had been a self-confessed fan of hers for some years. He had, at one time, even carried a travel bag adorned with her name, everywhere he had gone until the bag was stolen during his tour of Europe in 1992.

Not everyone, however, could be quite sure if the controversial, anguished musical genius was a serious admirer of her work or if his homage had more of an ironic twist to it. Whatever it was, they seemed poles apart in terms of image and style, despite having grown up in the same city only a few minutes away from each other, although their paths had never crossed.

Perhaps it was Kylie's honesty and lack of cynicism and ego that appealed to him most. Maybe, after his earlier spell in rehab trying to kick his heroin habit, and his tendency to find song material in life's gothic corners, he now yearned for a simpler way of life. His visit to Melbourne that year would certainly affirm that. Like Kylie, he enjoyed his Christmases at home with his family. And again, as with Kylie, it allowed him to retreat from public life.

From that point of view, Cave also felt an empathy towards Kylie's difficulties in shaking free from both the public and media perceptions of who she was, and more importantly, who she *should* be – though by now Kylie's sustained efforts to grow up were succeeding. She was doing everything within her power to rid herself of the wholesome guise with which *Neighbours* and PWL had saddled her, and while a couple of years earlier a collaboration with any of rock's lugubrious wild men might have left her looking ridiculous, these days she was no stranger to a darker side.

Since that time Cave had written many songs for Kylie – more out of sheer genuine admiration for her than anything else. And it wasn't until he discovered that both he and she were in town at the same time that he plucked up enough courage to approach Kylie with a view to her recording one of them.

Working on a project that would end up as *Murder Ballads* –
his most successful album to date – he had written a song for Kylie
to sing, deliberately low in key and very dark. He was far from
certain whether he would be able to persuade her to record it for
him, nor was he convinced that he would even have the courage to
ask her. All the same, it seemed too good an opportunity to pass up.

Deliberately steering clear of record company intrusion, he
had obtained the Minogue family's home phone number through
his bass player Mick Harvey, who in turn had got it from Michael
Hutchence. It was where Cave would finally attempt to contact
her directly, even though it would take several attempts before
the pair would finally connect.

Kylie recalls, 'I actually remember Michael Hutchence
saying, "My friend Nick wants to do a song with you." I didn't
know much about Nick Cave before I met him. I was in
Melbourne and Nick was in Melbourne at the same time and we
were on the same record label by this time, so the message came
through that he was interested in having me duet with him on
the *Murder Ballads* album.'

Kylie had received a tape and a note from Cave. The latter
invited her to give him a call to discuss working together; on the
former was a rough-cut of the song he had written for her, called
'Where The Wild Roses Grow'.

'He was leaving messages with my mum because I was staying at home with my parents, and I'd call back and leave a
message with his mum, so it wasn't rock 'n' roll like people would
expect,' Kylie today laughs at the memory.

'To cut a long story short, the day I recorded my vocals for
"Where The Wild Roses Grow" was the first day I met Nick, and I
think that added a lot to the song, to the tenderness and the
sexual tension and the frailty of that song.'

She didn't realise it at the time but following the slow transition to becoming an artist of more credibility through her work with deConstruction, 'Where The Wild Roses Grow' would become the point from which there was no turning back.

The melancholy waltz-time ballad was nothing like any of her previous recordings, but Kylie loved it from the start. True to Cave's reputation for pessimism and dark subject matter, it cast her in the role of tragic, virginal Eliza whose beauty and virtue drive her lover to violence and her to her death. The closing lines of the song had Cave bludgeoning Kylie's character to death with a rock beside a riverbank.

The mood and potential controversy that such a song might cause was irrelevant to Kylie. 'It was so good that I can't imagine my life or career without having done that song.'

The normally laconic Nick Cave found working with his idol amazing and the song's producer Victor Van Vugt was equally impressed by Kylie's attitude, as well as her musical ability. And Kylie herself? She found Nick Cave 'really gorgeous' and 'mild and gentle, very lovely'. Under his guidance she uncovered new dimensions in her voice. Following on from his friend Michael's influence years earlier, Nick had unleashed a new musical freedom in Kylie that she would never let go of.

The recording session also marked the start of an enduring friendship between Kylie and Cave, one which would be heightened by the success of the song later that year, and their live appearances together to perform and promote it.

In the meantime, Kylie had other things to think about. She had been given an unusual film script by a friend within weeks of her arrival home. The film, an Australian independent, was only 11 minutes long and would be made on the tiniest of budgets. With a pay cheque no more than the basic union rate, it was a ludicrous fee compared with the standards Kylie had come to expect. But the tough, challenging character she had been asked to play intrigued her so much, and with filming scheduled to last only over a week, how could she not accept?

*Hayride to Hell* would prove to be the most controversial and most removed role from her real self that Kylie had yet accepted, but it was just the kind of role Kylie had been looking for – something to get her teeth into. Her involvement with the project undoubtedly boosted the film's appeal no end and is probably why it received premiere screenings at the prestigious London Film Festival, the well-respected Chicago Underground Film Festival and the Telluride Festival in the American midwest, all leading art-house events. It would also see several outing on UK television over the following year.

Although the commercial circuit for the film was never a serious option, Kylie would still speak out in her own promotional interviews appealing for financial backing for the film.

For Kylie it proved not only the biggest challenge yet to her acting skills but one that also relied on some of the physical skills she had learned for *Street Fighter*. She played a psychotic quasi-drug addict who terrorises a motorist played by Australian actor Richard Roxburgh, on his way home from work.

There were some manic scenes with Kylie trying to strangle her co-star and jumping on and off a moving car, for which she was offered a stunt double by director Kimble Rendall, but she refused, instead taking on all the action herself. Rendall was simply amazed by her professionalism. For Kylie herself it was as if the world outside the film set ceased to exist for a week. She worked 14-hour days, and found it hard to switch the character off when she went home.

She also had the opportunity during her three-month visit home to co-host a live chat-and-variety show called *Denton*, which she used partly to plug the film. Although she had not been warned about the stunts and set-ups which formed an integral part of the evening, she did manage to sidestep them good-humouredly. She also found herself on the receiving end of some sharp-edged teasing by another bad boy from the music world. Slash, guitarist of the then popular rock band Guns 'N Roses waxed facetious on the subject of her limousine parked outside next to his battered van. In spite of such on-screen antics, she was swift to assure journalists that he couldn't have been sweeter to her behind the scenes.

That encounter set the scene for an even more abrasive confrontation with the guitarist a few months later when Kylie went backstage after watching Slash perform at a Sydney venue with his new band, Slash's Snakepit, when she would be dismissed as nothing more than a groupie. The problem may have had something to do with her new auburn hairstyle. Even her grandmother failed to recognise her at first when she changed from her familiar dark blonde, and for several weeks afterwards even her most ardent fans passed her in the street without a second glance.

But she had a reason for changing the colour and style. Not, as some may have thought to disguise herself, but for another movie role she had just landed on the back of her role in *Street Fighter*.

*Bio-Dome* was a comedy produced by Brad Krevoy, best known for the 1995 box-office smash *Dumb and Dumber* with Jim Carrey and Jeff Daniels in the title roles. For *Bio-Dome*, Kylie would play Petra, an Australian oceanographer, opposite actors Pauly Shore and Stephen Baldwin as a pair of goons who become trapped in the environment-controlled 'bio-dome' where she carries out her experiments and gets in the way of their work with predictable hilarity.

On set, Kylie and her manic co-star Shore were reported to have become lovers but the alleged affair was short-lived, as was Kylie's liking for the completed movie, and left Shore feeling bemused, as he made clear on his official website when speaking about his ex-girlfriends, Kylie clearly being classed as one of them.

There was a snapshot online under the heading of 'Me and Snoo' (his nickname for Kylie). The photo was taken in the Bahamas on an island called St Martin shortly after they finished filming. 'Kylie and I dated for about four months,' he says. 'She lives in London now, continuing her music career. That was a bad break-up. Here's what happened: I flew to London to see her and as I was flying there, she was flying to L.A. with her brand-new boyfriend, Stefane, a video director. Kylie and I haven't talked for a long time, so if any of you guys out there in England see her, tell her to fucking call me. Or at least email me.'

Although the movie looked good on paper, the bad Australian jokes and childish capers of the final cut proved even more discouraging than *Street Fighter*. 'You don't get to perform unless you're the star,' she objected. 'These Hollywood things are like, let's get her into something short and tight. I long to do an independent film where the scenes made sense and there was a story.' *Hayride to Hell* had clearly left a powerful impression.

Even though the movie fell short of her expectations, she was still feeling unfulfilled yet again. But she did have her music to return to. Although there was no word on plans for the Cave duet yet, and whereas some may have been thinking it would only receive a low-key Australian release at best, deConstruction had chosen a third single to release off the *Kylie Minogue* album.

Flying back to the UK before her stint in the US filming *Bio-Dome*, Kylie had heavily reworked 'Where Is The Feeling?' with Brothers In Rhythm, and it was now ready for release. The single proved to be her least commercial to date, with a sexily murmured verse, reworked from the bright and breezy vocal of the original, and thumping bass-heavy backing track. The release also featured some of her hardest remixes to date, gaining her another dose of credibility into the bargain. Although the release only reached Number 16 in the UK chart, it was critically acclaimed as yet another positive progression in Kylie's musical style.

The sleeve, video, and accompanying promotion all featured Kylie with her new red hair, dyed especially for her role in *Bio-Dome*. 'Same hair, different colour', she told Steve Wright, when he attempted to make a fuss of the change. The video, another steamy affair, filmed in a school swimming pool in Los Angeles, featured Kylie being pursued through the murky water by an ominous figure who turned out to yet be another strikingly built model.

*Bio-Dome*, meanwhile, did nothing to capture the American box-office audience it had hoped to attract. In Australia, the film by-passed the big screen and went straight to video, going on to sink into oblivion when it was eventually released in the UK.

With her promotional work finished on her album and with her experiences on both *Street Fighter* and *Bio-Dome* long forgotten, Kylie would spend a month realising a long-held dream of driving along the legendary Route 66, a journey her father had undertaken in his youth. She did so with a new friend, top French photographer Stephane Sedanoui whom she had just met. By the end of their journey, her new companion was the new man in her life.

'For a long time it had been on my mental list of things to do in life – drive across America', she remembers. 'And as it happened I fell in love on the way and ended up seeing him for a long time.'

Rumours that she was planning to stay in America and accept a role in the new, high-profile television soap series *Central Park* proved unfounded. After her holiday she gave up on movie stardom for the time being and returned to London, where she was sure of a welcome from her many gay fans at the annual Gay Pride festival. She took a crowd of over 3,000 by storm at the Astoria club in Soho, wearing the skimpiest of satin outfits which drew the comment from one fan that she seemed to have forgotten to put on her dress!

By the summer it was plain that *Kylie Minogue*, her first album for the deConstruction label, was not attaining the mega-sales of her earlier recordings; despite a gratifyingly approving reception from the critics its early success had tailed off, and the figures eventually reached only half a million – a far cry from the five million her PWL work had previously achieved, demonstrating, perhaps, that her new musical style had connoisseur rather than mass appeal.

Her ongoing association with Nick Cave helped to sustain this new sophisticated musical image. On her return to London in March she had joined him for further recordings on the *Murder Ballads* album, singing a few lines on his cover version of the Bob Dylan number 'Death Is Not The End', the closing track. In the meantime, 'Where The Wild Roses Grow' had been chosen as *the* single to be released from the album. And when they heard that news they both began work on the video.

The controversial clip was described as 'satanic' by some newspapers, although the label probably owed more to Nick

Cave's self-confessed obsession with the occult than to the actual content. It was shot at an unnamed stately home, and Kylie's role consisted mainly of lying in a river in skimpy white satin, depicting a corpse – though both Cave himself and a snake got to wrap themselves around her.

The high esteem in which Nick Cave held Kylie, and his willingness to express his views in public to anyone who asked, gave the biggest boost to her aspirations towards musical credibility since Michael Hutchence. Fans and critics alike found their views challenged as she revealed yet another new side to her talent and hinted that there were more surprises in store.

Along with a number of other deConstruction performers, she was booked to appear at two leading summer music festivals, the Feile at Cork in the Republic of Ireland and T in the Park in Glasgow. After performing 'Shocked', 'Better The Devil You Know' and 'Confide In Me', among others, she invited Cave to share the limelight with her, to perform their duet live at both events in front of thousands.

Afterwards Cave, well-known as a wild man of rock 'n' roll, was moved to confess to Kylie that being on stage with her had been one of the most terrifying experiences of his life. 'Nothing,' he told her, 'has ever made me as uncomfortable as singing to that pocket of Kylie Minogue purists who shook their fingers whenever I defiled your sacredness by touching you or holding your hands.' Kylie, of course, had felt the same when appearing at other live shows as Nick's guest.

A busy summer was followed by an even busier autumn, the highlight of which was a prestigious appearance at the Royal Albert Hall.

The occasion was Equality 95, a high-profile fundraising

concert organised by gay rights pressure group Stonewall in October. As one of the world's leading gay icons Kylie was invited to join such showbiz luminaries as Jennifer Saunders and Joanna Lumley, both with gay followings almost as large as her own; the flamboyantly camp Julian Clary; the recently outed Michael Barrymore; and of course the music business's foremost gay figure Elton John, with whom she would appear on the cover of the following month's *Gay Times* magazine, the UK's biggest and most credible gay publication.

More than 5,000 flocked to the event, and greeted Barrymore's rendition of the camp anthem 'I Am What I Am' with sympathetic cheers. But the highlight of the evening by a long stretch was Kylie's gloriously high camp duet with Elton John. She wore a minuscule tasselled pink bikini outfit; he was in fishnet stockings, Pamela Anderson style blonde wig, a black sequinned Versace dress and matching gloves. They sang 'Sisters Are Doing It For Themselves', and according to those present, the roof of the Albert Hall almost lifted off.

So what is it about Kylie that appealed so powerfully to the gay community then and still does to this day?

One fan put forward the theory that gay men have never quite left behind their teenage years, with all the baggage the term implies – not only the fun-loving irresponsibility, but the black depths of despair too.

'I certainly have that "adolescent-ness" about me,' he admits, his expression half-proud and half-wry. 'There's a period during adolescence that is miserable – all the more so when you're just coming to terms with being gay – because you can't talk or act the way you really want to. Kylie's music is an escape – bold, simple, sometimes a bit trite, but who cares! This is important when you're alone and feeling down – certainly for me. I think Kylie caught people at a certain time. I was entering my teenage years, and she and her music were comforting.'

Kylie herself shed a little light on the question in an interview with *Attitude*, the gay style magazine. When the interviewer asked her why she thought gay Britain loved her so much, Kylie was quick to respond

> aside from me being a show pony? There was a period when I was having knives dug into me from every angle, quite unnecessarily. As an eighteen-, nineteen-year-old girl I really had a problem figuring out why everyone was being so nasty and, on occasion, vindictive. There comes a point when you think, OK, so I've got a bad hairdo – yours ain't so hot either! Maybe it's a little crass, but I think gay people understand unnecessary criticism.

Maybe she is right but, continues the fan, 'Kylie is glamorous. She's beautiful. She has fun with her image, those constant changes. These are all attributes that gay men can associate with. I love watching her videos, her live shows, her interviews. She carries herself with an air of confidence. She sparkles. It's very appealing, and I think gay men like to feel some element of "fabulousness" about themselves. They may copy certain qualities about her – it's a kind of glamour by association.

'Have you ever seen a troupe of gay men doing the moves to one of her songs? I have, and while I personally find it amusing, I also secretly think, I wish I knew the moves!

'I think Kylie has adopted her fan base, and is loyal to them. She appears to have some sense of responsibility to her gay fans, and is not out to make money from them overtly as other teeny pop stars (and their management) seem to be. Kylie actively chooses to produce the kind of music that she does.'

By October 1995 the Kylie and Cave duet had hit the shops, and with it came critical acclaim in abundance. The track hit Number 11 in the UK, higher than most had predicted, and with it came two much talked about appearances on *Top Of The Pops*. Back home in Australia a Number Two chart placing followed.

'It was a special time,' Cave would tell *The Times* in April 2001, 'because we created that song without any intention of it being a hit, it just seemed like a good idea at the time.'

The next step for Kylie had to be a new album, to capitalise on the wave of freedom and creativity this new experience with Cave had brought about. Meetings with Brothers In Rhythm, the production duo who had worked wonders on the *Kylie Minogue* collection, had already taken place. Plans for the album were in progress – but that was for the future.

Meanwhile, 1995 had one more new development in store for Kylie and her fans. The October London Fashion Week invariably throws up some surprises. That year the media spotlight was turned on a certain young Australian singing star called Dannii Minogue, launching a designer collection for a leading department store.

Then there was up and coming designer Antonio Beradi, hailed as the British fashion scene's rising star and making his debut during the week. Upmarket supermodel Stella Tennant took on the task of showing his creations to advantage – and working alongside her was a diminutive novice to the catwalk.

Yes, Kylie had become a fashion model for the day, upstaging everyone in sight including her little sister. Her fiery hair was teased into a wild, punky style by Sam McKnight, better known for his attentions to Princess Diana's blonde locks; and the slinky, revealing outfit chosen for her by Beradi was slashed right down to the navel and held up by the flimsiest of lacing. And, raved everyone, she strode that catwalk to the manner born.

All in all, 1995 had been quite a year: romance, movies, another change in musical style leading to several steps up in the eyes of the hip music world; then a major gig at one of the world's leading venues, and a toe dipped into the completely alien waters of the designer end of the rag trade. 'Chameleon Kylie' was now her well-earned epithet.

Teen pop star was one image she had sloughed off for good. Nick Cave's influence gave Kylie more self-assurance than ever before; his support lent credibility to her music, and the confidence not just to leave the past behind but to thumb her nose at it with a high-profile ironic gesture. On 7 July 1996, less than a year after her show-stopping duet with Elton John, it was Cave who persuaded her to go on stage at the Albert Hall – but this time not as a singer, but a poet.

The event was the Poetry Olympics, a hip 24-hour marathon with a line-up which included master songwriter Ray Davies, Blur's Damon Albarn, singer Patti Smith and actress Nerys Hughes. Kylie told reporters, 'He said I should go out there and face my past, with whatever demons there might be.'

She recited the words of her first number one hit 'I Should Be So Lucky' in the grand manner of a Shakespearean soliloquy. It went down a storm, and the media got the message loud and clear.

'I tried to wriggle out of it in all kinds of ways,' she laughs. 'But Nick is clever. When I finally did it, it was a truly exhilarating moment.'

As always, rumours abounded in the press of a romantic connection with Cave, but were laughed off by all parties concerned; she was now well and truly attached to Stephane, someone who was about to influence her career further. Her devotion to all things French was no secret; Paris was one of her favourite cities, and she maintained a small, bohemian apartment there. She was seen in public with Sedanoui for the first time in the spring at a Tina Turner video shoot; while her new lover did his stuff behind the camera, she sported a new, cropped hairstyle and happily played the role of tea-making assistant.

The ultra-cool ponytailed Frenchman had been engaged to Icelandic singer Björk. But for the moment, blissfully happy though they were, marriage did not form part of their plans.

His influence led to another new look. In the second half of the year Kylie began to sport the style of unisex combat gear Sedanoui favoured, and became a slender brunette – so slender, in fact, that there was speculation about a return of the near-anorexia she had almost succumbed to back in the 1980s when stress almost got the better of her. One photographer who had snapped her through all her changes of image described her huge, black-circled eyes and said she looked like a skinny art student. Other friends wondered if she was becoming danger-ously obsessed with her weight, and an acquaintance in the music business fuelled the rumours with a suggestion that she played with her food instead of eating it. 'She's painfully thin at the best of times, and she's a very finicky eater,' he added.

Kylie denied it, vehemently and publicly. 'Anorexia is a state of mind, not just losing weight – I've always felt good and confi-dent about myself.' An attitude enhanced by being in love.

One possible explanation for the weight loss was a healthy eating programme Kylie was trying to follow. Never a fan of junk food, she was often seen buying fat and sugar-free snacks from Ernest Hilton at a Chelsea shop which promoted French chef

Michel Montignac's Eat Yourself Slim concept – a variation on the better-known Hay diet, based on the theory of not mixing certain types of food. 'Kylie probably doesn't cook much, so I expect she uses us to help her eat healthily,' Hilton explained.

The rumours were scotched in the December issue of the trendy magazine *I-D*. A revealing photo-spread showed Kylie stripping to the briefest of underwear in the back of a car as she changed clothes for the Hyde Park shoot – and though she was as slim and petite as ever, she was *not* anorexic.

Perhaps the press were so keen to focus on Kylie's physical attributes because she gave them little to comment on in a musical sense. Quietly working on a new album, she was keeping it all happening behind closed doors. Not one new song was heard throughout 1996.

But in December Kylie gave the public and music press a shocking indication of things to come. The Welsh cult band Manic Street Preachers, at that time the last word in cool, moody rock music, were performing gigs at the Shepherds Bush Empire in London in the run up to the Christmas period.

There had been vague rumours that Kylie had been working with them, but few had taken them seriously, as such stories had done the rounds once before. But just ten days before Christmas at one of the group's gigs, lead vocalist James Dean Bradfield invited a guest on to the stage midway through their set, and out came Kylie, dressed in jeans, tight black polo-neck and what *NME* described as 'her hair pegged up in a curious mohican'. She performed 'Little Baby Nothing', the 1992 track the Manics had originally written for Kylie to sing. Relaxed and confident, she received a warm reception from an astonished but interested crowd.

IndieKylie had truly arrived.

## TEN

# IMPOSSIBLE DREAM

By June 1997, when deConstruction were ready to add the final touches at the recording studio in Bath to Kylie's new album, initially titled *Impossible Princess,* it had already been in production for 21 months.

There had been many changes of direction and remixes in that time. Some co-writers had been dropped and others recruited even though Kylie herself had written or co-written every single track that ended up on the set. Although the project had been a long – and at times upsetting and infuriating – process, it was one that would eventually stand Kylie in good stead.

Again, it seemed as if the entire cream of the music business were on hand to take Kylie, this time, into a far more credible direction than she could ever have imagined. The collaborations alone were enough to earn her the new nickname of IndieKylie through the pages of Britain's most significant music press. And although Nick Cave had contributed a song that he called 'Soon', Kylie in one of her moments of panic felt she hadn't done the song justice and in the end decided it was best left to remake at a later date.

That would not be necessary for the two compositions she had written with James Dean Bradfield and the other guys from the Manic Street Preachers, and the authors of 'Little Baby Nothing', the hit song they had written about a helpless starlet, for which Kylie was said to have been the inspiration, and which she had performed with them on stage the previous Christmas.

The rumours of various highly credible collaborations had proven to be mostly true, and she was seemingly as thrilled to play the Sixties rock chick with the Manics as the breathy disco diva for Dave Ball, formerly of Soft Cell, and his partner Ingo Vauk, for her album. And if that wasn't enough to get her excited, then the involvement of Rob Dougan, from the label Clubbed To Death, was to be the icing on the cake.

Brothers In Rhythm, the producing duo from the cutting edge of dance music, who had been mainly responsible for her groundbreaking 1994 debut album for deConstruction, again worked closely with Kylie, but now more in developing her own creative ideas and songwriting. Adding music to some of Kylie's lyrics, they were the musical keystone for the project.

'On *Princess*, it was mainly up to us to embellish and add subtle lyric and melody ideas to her already existing plot,' remembers Steve Anderson, one half of the duo. 'Kylie's ideas are always unique and inspiring, which I believe comes across on this album.'

Indeed, all the material that was prepared and recorded was completely different from anything Kylie had ever done before. Techno, rock, dance, drum 'n' bass and trip-hop were just some of the different styles she incorporated. And as for her vocals, they were likened to Tori Amos, Björk, Sinead O'Connor, Kate Bush and Madonna, as well as her own inimitable self, of course. Chameleon Kylie it seemed was back again, adopting whatever role each song required of her. The only difference this time was that now she was writing her own script.

'I've learnt so much by doing this album,' Kylie confessed. 'It was like being in a park for the first time and not wanting to write about it before seeing it all, tasting it, lying in it, and breathing it in, in case I missed something. Consequently I went almost everywhere.'

The album was scheduled for release in September with August set aside for the first single, 'Some Kind of Bliss'. It was one of the tracks that had been recorded with the Manic Street Preachers and had fared exceptionally well on airplay. But even with such good reception and a general consensus that seemed destined to continue Kylie's run of chart success in the UK, the news that was announced one Sunday morning that same month left everyone barely able to contain their grief.

To many, it was unthinkable that Diana, Princess of Wales, had had her life cut short when she was tragically killed with Dodi Fayed – the playboy son of billionaire Mohammed Al Fayed – in a bizarre car accident in Paris. And with Kylie's single released in the week that followed the tragedy, it was no surprise that it should stall two places outside the Top Twenty before beginning its descent back down the charts again.

Despite the tragic loss of Diana, there were high hopes for the album, now hastily retitled *Kylie Minogue* from the previous and now deemed unsuitable *Impossible Princess*. Another setback, largely due to the poor charting of the single – and perhaps to the unfortunate timing as well – was the original

release date that would now be rescheduled for November alongside the second single.

Although Kylie was unwilling to subject herself to the high-
pressure publicity circus that had accompanied most of her early
hit records, to coincide with the album's new release date she did
agree to take on several interviews – one with *The Big Issue* – the
high-profile quality magazine which provides work and opportunities for homeless people.

In the feature that November, the article highlighted how far
she had travelled since those early days, how she became aware
that creativity comes from a person's dark side, how she had gone
in search of her own gloomier depths in order to write songs, but
had emerged with another kind of self-knowledge, and that she
didn't really have much of a dark side at all.

Certainly, she admits, 'I love to cry. I cry with frustration.
The first track on the album is as psychotic as I've been. I was
feeling overloaded, that everything had gone too far. I went for a
walk, then into a café and wrote it all down to get it off my chest.
I took the moment by the throat by putting it all on paper – it
was brilliant.'

Even though she had always been a paparazzi target right
from the early days, 1997 also saw her become something of a
favourite with broadsheet journalists as well, though none of
them would succeed in performing the hatchet job they would
probably have loved to do on her.

That was because, whatever their original intentions, they
all found her engaging and unpretentious, without a single
prima donna cell in her body. Not only journalists, but costume
makers, designers, anyone who came in contact with her, one
after another remarked, often against their will, on how *nice* she
really was.

They all found her cheerful, undemanding, co-operative, unassuming: the kind of girl who didn't make a fuss if there was no milk for her tea, but drank it black instead.

Asked if she had made mistakes, she admitted to an indiscretion or two in the past – the Galliano fishnet bodysuit, for instance, and the soft-porn photos published at the same time as her first deConstruction album. She still occasionally let herself be persuaded into something with a kitsch edge. For instance, earlier in the year she had made an entrance at a gig at a Melbourne casino by leaping from the mouth of a giant clam.

'I should have been born in the heyday of Hollywood,' she said, half wryly, half wistfully, 'and been the all-singing, all-dancing, all-acting, hey-I-can-skydive girl.'

There were still rumours of anorexia – Kylie Thinogue as the tabloids often dubbed her – and she admitted that for a while she had been underweight. 'I was too thin for a while because I was working very hard and getting stressed,' she explained.

'I wasn't happy with that; if I lose six pounds it's going to show.' But at the end of the interview with *The Big Issue*, she demanded to know where her lunch was. And as if to prove the point, the journalist who interviewed her for the *Telegraph Magazine* even watched her demolish pasta and crème brulée.

The media, tabloids and distinguished alike, had always given her a rollercoaster ride, yet the closest she came to grumbling about it was when she pointed out, 'Every time I do anything people say it's make-or-break time. Yet I carry on.' And she was right, of course.

The overall impression was that Kylie the tortured soul simply didn't exist. Perhaps her new-found love of songwriting was more cathartic than people realised, keeping her darker side removed from her public persona.

But Kylie's patience was about to be put to the test again – and this time it was too late to be exorcised through songwriting. The album – the promotion for which was being frantically reconsidered by deConstruction – was to be put back twice again, first to January of the following year and then eventually to March. Kylie's head was spinning.

Back home in Australia, of course, the album, still bearing its original title, was doing great business, so what better than to go off on a whirlwind promotional tour through her homeland to ensure the album continued to be successful. And it did. In fact, it remained on the Australian official ARIA chart for months on end.

There was only one blot on her landscape during her visit – the publication of an unauthorised biography by Dino Scatena that among other things discussed the loss of her virginity in a school cupboard. Whether she did or not, Kylie was not pleased. If she refused to acknowledge the book as if it didn't exist, then perhaps no-one else would either.

Out of the spotlight, of course, she was in love again. French photographer and now her boyfriend, Stephane Sedanoui created the look for the album's release and was largely responsible for the new, much talked about 'IndieKylie' image. Certainly, there was no denying his positive effect on her creativity. 'Stephane, merci, et je t'adore', she wrote in the album's credits. Not only that, but many of the featured song lyrics also stemmed from Kylie's apparent love for Stephane.

As if to prove the point, the second single from the album, 'Did It Again' – one of her own lyrics – even had a dark edge. It advocates confronting the monsters we create in our minds, and reveals a tougher, more complex Kylie than any of her earlier songs.

Certainly, deConstruction went all out on the video, in a second attempt to give Kylie a boost prior to her album's release. The self-mocking video featured four Kylies, Cute, Sex, Dance and IndieKylie, battling it out with chairs, bottles and baseball bats for the title of Queen Of Pop. With tongue firmly in cheek, IndieKylie won out.

The track, which she heavily promoted on UK television, fared a little better than 'Some Kind of Bliss'. It peaked at Number 14 and stayed in the chart for another six weeks.

Stephane Sedanoui remained on the scene throughout the ups and downs with the album, even though there was talk of quarrels and disagreements, but then again, what relationship is perfect? All the same, their dating would encourage the usual run of tabloid tales of wedding bells and babies.

Kylie's relationship with Stephane was aided by state-of-the-art communication technology. His work took him around the world and when away the most convenient method to stay in touch was by e-mail. It was probably what gave Kylie the excuse to develop her passionate devotion to the Mac PowerBook she now proudly owned. Even if she was free of commitments, she never thought twice about getting on a plane to fly thousands of miles so that they could be together. Aside from her Mac, travel, she once said, was her greatest self-indulgence.

Although they spent very little time actually living together, Kylie continued to share her Chelsea flat with a girlfriend, and was often pictured enjoying some of the benefits of a single life. More often than not, she could be spotted casually dressed with no make-up, wandering around London's street markets in search of bargains.

She was also approaching her thirtieth birthday, and though the absence of any children of her own remained a source of sadness for her, she had at the same time discovered self-reliance. She also learned to choose men more discerningly. Stephane had his own career, game plan and success record, and did not depend on her in any way at all. Without question their relationship was one of equals.

'I believe that you are on your own,' she told *The Big Issue*. 'People come together for a while then go their separate ways again.' She even told one journalist that she felt lucky. 'There are buskers on the streets who are better than me. I was just born under a lucky star.'

But the luck, it seemed, was about to run out.

Her singles had fared less well than in previous years, and delays with the album rolled painfully on. By late October, the relationship with Stephane Sedanoui, her second great love, came to an end. It was hard to tell if she was philosophical about it or just professional. Her reaction was to put on her make-up, take a deep breath and get on with her life. She even agreed to an interview with a leading newspaper just days after they split.

'I'm not grieving,' she told the *Express*. 'Stephane and I had some great times, but people grow in different directions, don't they?'

But there was much worse news in store. Just a few weeks later, Kylie was woken at 4 am one morning by the phone call everyone dreads: a friend in Australia was calling to break the dreadful news that her good friend and ex-lover Michael Hutchence had been found dead in a Sydney hotel room, in bizarre circumstances that would probably never be fully explained. Michael was the first person close to her to die, and Kylie was knocked sideways. 'It seemed totally surreal,' she said later, still wondering quite what had hit her.

As well as family and friends from the music world, a host of fans appeared at the funeral in St Andrew's Cathedral in Sydney. Kylie was one of a procession of Michael's exes, all clearly devastated by his death; Danish supermodel Helena Christensen was there, and his last partner television presenter Paula Yates, mother to his daughter Heavenly Hiraani Tiger Lily. Paula had tried to bar Australian actress Kym Wilson, the last person to see him alive, from the ceremony, but without success.

Indeed, Kylie was not alone in paying homage to Hutchence's image and preferences. Her decision to break from tradition and wear funeral black with plunging necklines and high heels was duplicated by several of the line-up of exes.

Fellow Australian rock star Nick Cave was among the music figures there to pay their respects, as was Tom Jones. He had interrupted his hectic Australian touring schedule to put in an appearance at the church.

Overall, it was probably the saddest day of Kylie's life, but it had its theatrically gothic moments. Recalling the occasion in an interview a couple of years later, Kylie described how thunder and rain arrived exactly on cue as the coffin came out of the cathedral. 'You couldn't have scripted it better,' she declared.

The consensus was that charismatic, hedonistic Hutchence had packed a full life into living the years he had. For Kylie he had been a turning point. 'He opened my eyes to the ways of the world. I would not have missed our relationship for anything – and I miss him.'

With 1997 almost behind her, Kylie looked positively on the coming year. She still had an album to release and with it all the attendant publicity duties that it would entail. She was also heading towards a watershed birthday, her 30th on 28 May.

The approach of such an occasion encourages everyone reaching that milestone to do some hard thinking and as 1998 began Kylie must have been looking towards May with an eye on her biological clock. Babies had always been part of her life-plan, and the end of her two-year relationship with Stephane Sedanoui meant that her wish to start her own family was back on hold again.

But the media, always preoccupied with her love life, seemed determined to turn every date into a serious affair. In January it was William Baker, a student she met while out shopping in Vivienne Westwood's eccentric fashion store a few years earlier. Theirs was a friendship which had turned into a productive working alliance. Simply put, she liked his ideas, and he would soon leave Westwood's employ to become Kylie's stylist.

'I was working in the Vivienne Westwood store in London part-time and bored,' remembers Baker. 'One day I called deConstruction and asked if she had a stylist, left my name and number and where I was calling from and thought nothing more of it. I had had absolutely no styling experience before, and it really wasn't something I had always thought about, but I had kind of been fascinated with her for some time, ever since I saw her doing the ironing in the "What Do I Have To Do" clip. It was strange, but I just felt drawn to her. Anyway, they said they would pass the message on to her as she was out of the country, and about three weeks later she came into the store. I leapt from behind the counter and bombarded her with ideas and somehow persuaded her to go for a coffee.'

Later that same year, Baker would shine as he and Kylie co-designed the glamorously kitsch set for her concert tour. As for his supposed romantic interest in Kylie, the media, of course, failed to notice that Baker had more of an eye for one of Kylie's strapping male dancers than for Kylie herself.

But that would not be enough to put the tabloids off for long. In February, Kylie was spotted in the VIP Red Room of Browns, the exclusive London nightclub, in a clinch on a sofa with Jay Kay, the flamboyant front-man of chart-topping band Jamiroquai, who discarded his eccentric headwear for the occasion. Not that a smoochy evening was a big deal. Jay Kay had split with his lingerie model girlfriend Tamsin Greenhill a few months earlier, so they were both free agents, so to speak. Although a friend told the press that Jay Kay had 'fancied her like mad', it appeared that the feeling was only fleetingly mutual. Probably feeling hurt by the rejection, Kay would later go on to criticise Kylie in the national press.

One month later, and now back in Australia, it was a different story entirely. Photographers had captured her on a naturist beach in Byron Bay, a cult resort in New South Wales. As far as that story went, she was apparently sharing a tent with male model Brent Waring when the house they were to accommodate with friends turned out to be full.

And then in the spring, Kylie was seen around town more than once with slapstick funny man and wild card Jim Carrey, the star of such blockbuster movies as *The Mask* and *The Truman Show*. But it soon became clear the two were a long way from being a couple as their meetings didn't exactly qualify as intimate dates. Carrey just wanted someone to talk to. The multi-millionaire comic actor was trying to bring about a reunion with his ex-wife Lauren Holly, but in a heart-to-heart with Kylie he confided that he was having second thoughts.

By the summer, Australian actor Daniel Lapaine, best-known for his role in *Muriel's Wedding* was briefly in the frame for a while, after he was identified as the mystery man she had, according to a tabloid journalist, snogged in the back of a taxi.

If all the stories were to be believed following the end of her romance with Sedanoui, Kylie had clearly decided to have some fun. And why not? She even admitted in a high-profile interview that when she wasn't in a steady relationship she enjoyed one-night stands, because, she claimed with a grin, they were cheaper than therapy. 'It's not something I frown on,' she admits. 'Although I've always been very choosy who I have sex with.

'I've never thought about marrying anyone,' she continued (though sister Dannii had told the press that she and Sedanoui were giving serious thought to marriage and kids). 'It doesn't appeal to me. I prefer to have different people at different times of my life.

'I love being in love. When I have a boyfriend I'm always faithful. But when it's over I don't think of it as failure. I prefer to remember what was good. I never expect relationships to last. That's probably one reason why I don't fall out with my boyfriends.'

Maybe that was true. But equally true was how the bizarre death of her former lover Michael Hutchence at the end of 1997 was put under the spotlight once again. 'The break-up was obviously the right thing to do,' Kylie declared. 'I'd have burnt out if I'd lived his rock 'n' roll lifestyle for too long.

'We'd all be very lucky if we could experience a man as charismatic, wise, sexy and funny as Michael,' she explains. 'When he died I was dumbstruck. I still think about him a great deal; it's made me cherish the time we had together. I often feel his presence.'

In the same interview she said it was in her nature to be flirtatious and an exhibitionist. Further evidence if any were needed of her chameleon tendencies, perhaps.

She was certainly in no hurry to settle into another long-term relationship. 'Being single suits me at the moment,' she was adamant. 'I take the reins a lot of the time. I like to choose whether or not I want to be in control. Falling in love is brilliant. I'd miss it more if I wasn't so busy.'

She would probably be the first to admit that the demands of her career left her very little time for a personal life for the first half of the year. She was again working hard to ensure that her overdue new album would now be received with as much exposure as possible.

Much to her pleasure, the album finally went on release in the UK in March 1998. Music critics and fans alike were keen to see how this latest change of image panned out. The song lyrics were, of course, all Kylie's own work, and some of them were dark and troubled. The moody and sophisticated collection provoked the reaction from the music press that she was a blank canvas waiting for other people to print their message on her.

'Beautiful but somehow helpless, unguided,' said one critic. 'Over-complicated, and never establishes a real mood,' averred another. Then again, on the other hand, Q magazine would go on to reassess the album long after its disappearance from the charts. 'This is proof that sales and quality aren't always linked,' shouted the magazine. 'No. Really ... Possibly one of the sexiest pop albums ever made.'

Some quarters had failed to identify with the new, more intimate Kylie, claiming that what she did best was still the flamboyant, upbeat showgirl numbers – that this was where her natural talent lay, and that the dark, serious side was best left to others.

Kylie's career began to look seriously in trouble that spring. Not even her most loyal supporters could claim that the album sold well, and 'Some Kind of Bliss' and 'Did It Again', the two singles from it released in 1997, had fallen a long way short of the huge success she had achieved with her earlier work. A third single 'Breathe', fared slightly better, released alongside the album, but again failed to break the Top Ten. At the same time, the critics also failed to remember the minor success she achieved with her later PWL releases, the final two singles faring no better than these. They did, however, have critical praise piled upon them, which could never have applied to her singles on PWL.

Even more damaging was the news that the album made just 10 per cent of the expected sales figures, with only 20,000 copies sold in the first two weeks. That was when demand was expected to peak. Although it made Number 10 in the album chart for one week, it rapidly dropped out of the Top 40, gaining just 47,000 sales, unlike the first PWL release, which sold two million copies and stayed in the charts for 67 weeks. However, it charted higher than her final and most critically acclaimed studio album for PWL, *Let's Get To It*.

But, of course, the press was now hounding her again, and as far as they were concerned things were just getting worse and worse for Kylie. Just a few weeks later record producer Ray Hayden's copycat claim reached court. The claim alleged that 'Confide in Me', Kylie's debut single with deConstruction back in 1994 and a huge hit, included a ripped-off chorus melody of his reworked version of 'It's A Fine Day'. Although Hayden lost his case, the stress and media attention of it all was yet another sting in the tail.

And as far as Kylie was concerned that was the end; everything had gone too far. Far more important, she determined, was the need to release herself from the constant media pressure that surrounded her; to consider how to get through it all with the minimum of scars. In every interview she gave at the time she quickly tired of having to defend herself against the 'IndieKylie' nickname that she had now been tagged with; and constantly having to explain the delays and problems surrounding the release of the *Impossible Princess* album. She also needed to turn what was becoming a nightmare into something more positive. If her only protection was flight and her only thought was of escape, then she had the answer. And as she reflected on her decision once she'd settled on her next move, instinct kicked in.

# ELEVEN

# LOVE TO YOU ALL

The moment Kylie stepped on to the runway tarmac at Melbourne airport, her world changed. She was stunned and delighted by the display of support that greeted her arrival.

Added to this was the fact that her latest album, still titled *Impossible Princess* in her homeland, was being hailed as the best and most successful work she had ever produced, and was fast heading towards Platinum status on Australia's official ARIA album charts. Leaving the pressures of Europe behind, Kylie had come home to acknowledge that fact gratefully and say thank you.

Another reason may have been that she was no longer part of what Australian showbusiness termed the tall poppy syndrome. It was almost customary for Australians to allow their stars to shine as brightly as they could during their climb up the ladder of success, but the moment they outgrew their status or ego, they could be cut back to size – and it was something Kylie had suffered from ever since her early days in *Neighbours*.

Even today, Kylie doesn't expect any you-are-a-goddess treatment. This was evident from the time when Madonna had adorned Kylie's name across her chest. 'To see my name on her T-shirt was surreal, it was great,' Kylie remembers. 'I've only ever met her at the MTV Awards where she wore the T-shirt. The first thing I think I said was "Hi! Nice to meet you." She asked me if I liked the T-shirt and I said, "Yes, I do like the T-shirt, thank you." The whole thing just had her savvy. But I did appreciate the sign of solidarity.'

Even more interesting was the fact that Madonna had expressed a love for Kylie's *Impossible Princess* album. So much that her record label Maverick had apparently even tried to sign up Kylie for America.

With the so-called rivalry and comparisons between Kylie and Madonna finally laid to rest, returning home during the first half of 1998, Kylie found things had changed quite dramatically. Her enduring fame had naturally preceded her and in the process she had become the best ambassador her home country could have hoped for, to the extent that she was seen as Australia's very own version of royalty. Contrary to what the album title suggested, she was very much a *possible* princess.

'I think I've had more flowers than ever before,' she said on her arrival. 'In Melbourne I felt like the Homecoming Queen. Everywhere I went it was welcome back. It sounds very cheesy and corny, and all of that, but it's just what you say when you're in your hometown – its great to be home.'

'It's good to have her back in the country, where she belongs,' agreed a reporter.

By the time Kylie had arrived back on home turf from London, she already knew how to present her appreciation to Australia. As far as she was concerned nothing could be better than a countrywide concert tour, only this time she wanted a more intimate feel so that she could be *up close and personal* with as many of her devoted fans as possible. And it was because of that approach that the Intimate & Live tour would prove to be one of the best experiences in Kylie's working life so far.

It would also be her first full-scale return to touring in seven years. Not until now did she feel that she had learned enough at the deConstruction label to be able to offer something new with a live show and do it justice.

'I think back to when I did it in '90 and '91, and it's so different, so much better,' she observed halfway through the tour. 'I think it's a lot more enjoyable because I'm a bit more relaxed, I've got my own material that I'm doing, and even though I haven't done concerts of this scale in a long time, I've done other little different things that have all helped to give me experience. Like with Nick Cave, Manic Street Preachers and Elton John – really varied performances. Actually, the Mardi Gras has influenced this show a lot.'

With concert dates announced for May and June, they immediately sold out to tens of thousands of enthusiastic fans, some travelling hundreds of miles and others even quitting their jobs in order to attend every show possible.

Although many extra performances were added to the original tour schedule it still wasn't enough to satisfy the demands of those wanting to see Kylie in person and to welcome her home in style. Every night ended the same way with multiple standing ovations and thunderous applause that brought the house down at each venue she played. In fact, it became such a regular occurrence that Kylie would often have to continue endlessly with the encores to keep the audiences happy.

'The fans were amazing,' Will Baker remembers. 'There were some who went to every single show and were in the front row every night. I gave a few cowboy hats that I'd, painstakingly I may add, covered in silver glitter and sequins, out on the last night, just because in a way they were part of the whole family feel.'

Indeed, it was the overwhelming attention from the fans that forced the Intimate & Live project to take on a whole new dimension. To satisfy as many people as possible, the tour would be extended to become not only concerts, but also to take in record signings, television, radio and magazine interviews, and most importantly a documentary for Australia's Channel Ten, the same network that had been responsible for picking up *Neighbours* after it had been axed by their rivals.

For the next two months Kylie would be followed round by a camera crew, cutely dubbed 'KylieCam' to capture her at functions, parties, film interviews, and of course, sneak around backstage before and after the shows as well as shooting footage from the actual concerts – all to be assembled later, cut and edited into a two-hour special suitable for television programming.

As usual Kylie worked together with friend and now her creative collaborator Will Baker on the concept for the show, one which would feature many surprises.

'Basically the whole show was meant to be a reflection and celebration of who Kylie is and what she represents, interpreted in our own inimitable style!' reflected Baker. 'Kylie has all these alter-egos that she flirts with from time to time; the showgirl, the stripper, the cowgirl, the rock slut and we wanted to explore all of these mini personalities in their own separate environments, all within the context of a live show.'

Influenced by Stephane's imagery for the *Impossible Princess*, album, the show opened with a huge video screen featuring Kylie's eyes examining the gathered crowd, before she emerged from the rear of the stage in the multicoloured cocoon from the album sleeve.

The first segment of the show featured IndieKylie. 'What I wouldn't do for a deep breath inside,' she murmured on 'Too Far', performed head to toe in black, just her and the band with no unnecessary glitz.

For her torch-song rendition of 'I Should Be So Lucky', however, things changed, and she was soon belting out Abba's 'Dancing Queen' in full showgirl attire, pink headdress and all the trimmings that go hand in hand with such a costume. 'She practically has her own dressing room,' Kylie laughs about the outfit. Certainly, her new role as Showgirl Kylie had arrived, one which would follow her into the next stage of her career. But for now, she was still experimenting, and was delighted by the ease with which everything had come together on stage.

'Watching musicians usually associated with John Farnham getting their teeth into breakbeats, and doing "Dancing Queen" and absolutely loving it was an absolute joy!' said Steve Anderson of Brothers In Rhythm in an exclusive interview with Internet fansite LiMBO. As more or less expected, he was Kylie's one and only choice of musical director for the tour.

As for the remainder of the show, the audiences were on their feet throughout, with Kylie playing a fantastic mixture of material old and new. She even took five minutes out to perform a demo song called 'Free' which would never see the light of day in a recording studio – something which would have been unthinkable during previous tours.

The end of the show featured an extended and rousing version of Kylie's anthem 'Better The Devil You Know' with glitter shooting into and over the audience for the finale. Indeed, 'If in doubt, apply more glitter' was the tour slogan. Whether Kylie, dancers, band and crew, or fans, it worked wonders, sending everyone away delighted.

'The glitter got everywhere!' recalls Will Baker. 'It was on people's faces, in their hair. I found it in my pubes. Such is the price of glamour!'

The shows won Kylie the best reviews of her career with many commenting on the amazing strength of her performance and vocals and of the true style that she now displayed live on stage. Not surprising really when you consider how significantly she had matured as a person, and more importantly, as a consummate performer. As was evident from the acres of press and television coverage she received in the weeks that followed the concerts.

'The show was simply the most unbelievable, educational and fulfilling thing I've ever been involved with so far,' raved Steve Anderson. 'It proved beyond any doubt what a stunning performer Kylie is and she rocked every night! It was especially rewarding to see this sell out and kick off in England too.'

Indeed, the tour ended with three nights at London's Shepherd's Bush Empire, on the very stage where she had stood alongside Manic Street Preachers just 18 months earlier. Although initially there had been no plans to take the show across to the UK as the whole project had been set up as an Australian only affair, the sheer pressure from British fans to bring over what they had been hearing about forced Kylie and her management to relent, and to perform three scaled down shows in London.

'It lost something in London due to the constraints of the venue,' Will Baker recalls. 'But it still seemed to work. We couldn't fit everything on to the backdrop, and there wasn't the budget to ship everything from Oz, so we had to drop some elements, and some of the replacements were just a little shabby. We had to replace the illuminated stripper's podium from 'Cowboy Style' with just a low table covered in glitter wrapping paper. There was almost a Spinal Tap quality to it all.'

Before the visit back to British shores, there had been plenty to keep Kylie occupied in between gigs. Record signings in HMV stores around Australia had seen crowds of thousands squashed into shopping malls to catch a glimpse of their very own princess and to have their album sleeves signed if they were lucky enough.

She had also become involved with the children's charity 'Kidshelpline'. She took part in advertising campaigns to increase public awareness and publicly talked about their work. Even though she did not have enough time to dedicate to the organisation as she would have liked, her involvement helped them immeasurably. The night she publicly announced her involvement with them was also the night Victorian Premier Jeff Kennett had awarded Kylie a 'Plaque Of Victoria' at a State reception held in her honour. Chock-a-block with Kylie's family and friends, the reception quickly made every one of the evening news bulletins around Australia.

'You have retained your freshness,' declared Kennett, a self-confessed Kylie fan. 'That you have retained your vigour, and you have come back to us, Australia, on this tour, is very much an inspiration.' Although Kylie was clearly moved by such a public honour, she could only say how overwhelmed she felt.

While touring Australia she also celebrated another landmark – her 30th birthday. 'One of the best presents I got was a dragster bike from a friend of mine,' Kylie raved. 'And yes, in true birthday-girl fashion, I will make the most of the opportunity and have another party in London.'

There were flowers, flowers and more flowers, messages from fans on the Internet, and a rousing on-line chorus of 'Happy Birthday' from friends and family on the stroke of midnight; she would also hear the crowd repeat the song at almost every gig she performed, even weeks after the special occasion had passed. 'It's the longest birthday I've ever had,' she laughed. Appearing to relish entering her 30s, she also noted that this decade was the best in any woman's life, while men go 'a little peculiar!'

Although it was inevitable that some members of her following would try to get more than their fair share of Kylie's attention during the Australian tour, Kylie did her best to stop and speak to fans waiting after each show, handing out auto-graphed postcards as she arrived and left the stage door of each venue, but anyone rudely pushing their way to the front of queues or literally *demanding* her attention was something she refused to tolerate.

One fan in particular, a drag queen, had become something of a nuisance. After pestering her all evening at a post-show party, he became quite bitchy about her ability to shoot pool; eventually Kylie's composure cracked, and drawing on her martial arts training from *Street Fighter*, she showed him who was in charge by wrapping a pool cue around his throat. The inci-dent did Kylie's standing no harm at all – if anything it enhanced her 'incredibly nice but totally in control' persona.

As a climax to the tour, Kylie was presented with the keys to the city of Melbourne, her birthplace and still the town she calls home.

After months of hard work, ending with the London shows and

work on a live album and video of the Intimate & Live tour at
Peter Gabriel's Real World studios in Bath, Kylie decided it was
time to take a break. Heading off to St Tropez, the South of
France's ritziest hotspot for a few days on the beach with a new
beau, she knew she had done the right thing and so did her
friends and family.

The latest man in her life wasn't a completely new face,
however. She had dated wealthy Tim Jefferies, grandson of the
Green Shield Stamp tycoon Richard Tompkins and owner of a
Mayfair photo gallery, briefly before Stephane Sedanoui stole her
heart. Jeffries seemed to have a particular liking for Australian
girls. After a brief marriage to Koo Stark, the actress, ex-model
and one-time girlfriend of Prince Andrew, he also had a three-
year romance with another Australian model, Elle MacPherson.

By the autumn of that year, Kylie had another new image to
unveil – Chameleon Kylie – but this one was made out of wax.
Her *Neighbours* era likeness had been part of the famous line-up
at Madame Tussaud's waxworks museum since 1989 and was way
out of date. It had actually been Tussaud's most touched – and
consequently damaged – figure and in early October 1998 an
updated figure was put on show to replace the vintage model.

The new-look Kylie, sporting an elegant upswept hairstyle and
a black lace slip, cost the museum £25,000, but they considered
the money well spent. 'Only a handful of figures are ever replaced,'
reinforced one of the museum's spokespersons. 'Kylie has changed
so much that it's worth every penny; she's still so popular.'

During the same month the waxwork had gone on display, Kylie
was having problems with the deConstruction label. She continued to be released on FMR in Australia, previously Mushroom,
with 'Cowboy Style' as her latest offering. It was another single

from her last album with a video that featured an on stage performance of the song filmed in rehearsals.

In the meantime, while the troubles at deConstruction rumbled on, they also put out a series of remix albums made up from a mountain of rare and unreleased material from her time with Stock Aitken Waterman. But it was the Intimate & Live packages that suffered the most. Without any UK release in sight, the album and video would only be available on import, and in the process, needless to say, topped the UK import charts.

At that time, her latest release in the UK was a compilation album of remixes from the *Impossible Princess* singles by some of the highest profiled club DJs. As if to emphasis Kylie's iconic status, the sleeve featured a simple but subtle silhouette of Kylie's figure, but no actual picture of her. Although the album would clearly not score many chart points, and maybe was never intended to, the whole thing seemed nothing more than a solution to Kylie's contractual obligation for a required third deConstruction album.

Shortly after, Kylie vowed to make her appreciation for her loyal Australian label quite clear when she agreed to be the opening act at the massive Mushroom 25th Anniversary concert held at the MCG Stadium in Melbourne. Dressed in black wig and geisha-themed costume, she began by singing 'Happy Birthday' à la Monroe to Mushroom and its chief Michael Gudinski, before bursting into a 25-minute medley of her hits, surrounded by a stage full of dancers. Although suffering from laryngitis and struggling to sing at some points, she carried on, humbly asking the crowd to help her out – and did Mushroom proud.

By this time the internal set-up at deConstruction appeared to be in trouble. The rumour was that the label was to be closed down in all but name, and form a subsidiary of its parent company BMG UK. Although Kylie was one of the last to depart the record company, her album and single 'Breathe' were still the biggest sellers for the label of that year.

Although much speculation surrounded the change of the label's future, it was said in one tabloid that Kylie was all but ready to call her music career quits even though nothing could have been further from her mind. In another, it was suggested that she was planning to follow in the footsteps of her sister. Unlike Kylie, when Dannii was dropped from her record label, she joined the London cast of the West End stage musical *Grease* and she has, with the exception of a new single here and there, continued to travel that path.

Even if there was some truth in the rumours, it would certainly not be a replacement for Kylie's plans to record a follow-up album to *Impossible Princess*.

Eventually, of course, Kylie and deConstruction did call it quits. Maybe the label had hoped for bigger sales from their new star signing. And perhaps, following the series of unexpected turns and setbacks, and deConstruction's apparent inability to market Kylie, the results fell short of what they had set their sights on.

Even with her new cool image giving Kylie the best musical credibility she'd had so far in her career, it was not enough to sell records – at least not in the same huge numbers that her previous singles and albums had. Plain economic sense took over from the fact that Kylie alone was not enough to keep the deConstruction label going. The company's sense of failure in not being able to do justice to Kylie must have been considerable.

By the time the news of their parting became public knowledge, Kylie was already back at work with her *other* career in acting. Capitalising on the huge welcome she had enjoyed in her home country earlier in the year, she accepted two roles in a couple of new Australian movies and at the same time was also considering a third for an American film project.

The first of the Australian ones was *Sample People*. It would feature Kylie in one of the lead roles playing Jess – a nightclub owner who becomes involved in a number of various scams. With a very low budget for production, it was never going to enjoy a wide release outside Australia, but this didn't bother Kylie. She was just pleased to be enjoying the experience of returning to work as an actress. She would even find herself recording a new song for its soundtrack called 'The Real Thing' with Josh Abrahms – the strength of which almost forced her Australian label to release it as a single.

The second movie, *Cut*, was slightly different in that it was not a lead role but a cameo appearance in the opening sequences of the film. Described as the Australian version of Wes Craven's popular slasher flick *Scream*, Kylie played the part of an ill-mannered and vindictive movie director who is promptly and brutally murdered by having her tongue cut out.

There were also other projects waiting in the wings. One of the most important things to take care of for Kylie and manager Terry Blamey was the offers that were now flooding into her office from many of the UK's biggest record labels.

Besides that Kylie had already recorded a duet, a cover version of 'The Reflex' with Australian singer Ben Lee for an Australian Duran Duran tribute album. The track, produced by Lee, was bright and breezy, with Kylie sounding excited to be back in the recording studio. Not surprisingly, it ended up as the album's biggest marketing cut on its release in Australia.

Kylie had also started to take stock of her career up to this point, and was determined to create something that would, once and for all, shake off any last vestiges of her past demons. Together with stylist Will Baker she decided upon a retrospective look at Kylie through the pages of a purely photographic book, which would prove to be an amazing look at her history when it was finally published the following year. Although planned as a limited edition coffee-table work, demand for the publication forced a reprint more or less as the first edition was made available. All proceeds from the £25 price were donated to three charities that held a particular interest for Kylie.

The book, a weighty bright pink tome, covered her whole life from childhood to more outrageous offerings such as the notorious picture taken by French photographers Pierre et Gilles back in 1995. It showed Kylie dressed up as a nun astride a carousel horse with legs exposed out of the pulled-up-to-her-thighs habit. But not all the photographs depicted unalloyed glamour. Some shots showed her having a bad day, others harked back to the early days of her fame, complete with puffball skirts and permed-locked haircuts.

Images were submitted by Bono, Jason Donovan, sister Dannii, footwear designer Manolo Blahnik, artist Sam Taylor-Wood, and a whole list of credible artists and photographers. On the professional side, credits were attributed to her former lover Stephane Sedanoui, and some of the fans who had assisted with the book's compilation, and old friends such as Bert Stern and Katerina Jebb.

Jebb had masterminded the controversial coffee-table book of photos published in 1994 when Kylie had posed for one or two completely nude shots, one of which showed a prone Kylie face down on a studio floor, but no-one apart from herself and her close circle of friends would ever be privy to them. And certainly, she said, they would never be published.

But clearly she had changed her mind; here those same shots were in a major new book. Naturally enough, it was the nude shots which attracted attention and caused controversy. They were all very tastefully done, but nonetheless Kylie appeared as nature intended. She was also criticised for having become self-indulgent by putting together a book all about herself. A little vain, perhaps? suggested one interviewer.

'Well, yes,' she responded disarmingly. 'But something of celebrity is self-centredness, the rest is insecurity. I change characters when I do a photo-shoot. I'm like the eight-year-old with the dressing-up box. It's kind of avoiding being me – rather than being captured, I become a new character and let that take over.'

Kylie's success at the London Fashion Week three years earlier had also borne unexpected fruit: in the last few weeks of 1998 images of a scantily clad Kylie were stopping traffic on billboards and buses all over Europe.

Perhaps the advertisers were inspired by a photo-spread in the men's glossy magazine *FHM* earlier in the year, which included shots in revealing black Janet Reger lace, a transparent little Agent Provocateur number and, in one surprisingly tasteful shot, nothing at all. But whatever spurred them on to do so, the trendy Swedish fashion giant H & M Hennes chose her to model their Christmas collection – a range of deliciously slinky underwear, including bra-and-briefs sets in burgundy and silver satin and deep red lace.

The pictures for the campaign were taken in Paris by Kylie's long-time friend Ellen von Unworth; the abandoned poses and tumbled hair made her a dead ringer for Marilyn Monroe, and again Kylie was all over the tabloids in the UK and at home. Contrary to some claims, her appeal was far from over.

Certainly, it had been an eventful year; some doors had

closed, but many others had opened. Now thirty years old, it looked as if Kylie was moving into yet another phase of her life; the chameleon had already changed her colour a few times, and was all set to take on a completely new image. By the time 1999 approached, she was already in discussions about something so different from any of her previous roles that the only possible reaction was astonishment – Kylie was about to become a Shakespearean actress.

An actor for most of her life, she was returning to her first love. Only this time it wouldn't be in front of a camera, but treading the boards as Miranda in Shakespeare's *The Tempest* in Barbados, of all places – and acting on a stage, Kylie would discover, was not like filming.

All the same, she turned up for rehearsals halfway through February, having already learnt her lines as thoroughly as any of her songs. The production was the brainchild of raconteur, impresario and showbiz genius Kit Hesketh-Harvey, the enterprising half of the camp cabaret double-act, Kit and the Widow. But what attracted him to *The Tempest* was simple. Although many in his place would have been initially reluctant to take on such a project, he was just bursting with enthusiasm. Not only that, but the play, put on now, he felt could be heralded as a production for an era when the exoticism of the Caribbean had just begun to filter through the English consciousness.

The production was the highlight of the Virgin Atlantic Holders Season, an annual drama and opera festival which takes place on the seventeenth-century Barbados plantation of billionaire and society host, Jodie Kidd's father, John. Among others who had performed there were Luciano Pavarotti and Lesley Garrett.

Hesketh-Harvey's first choice as director and star was Peter O'Toole, one of the most flamboyant, crowd-pulling figures ever to walk the boards, but cast and crew alike were paid in sunshine, appreciation and pocket money, and O'Toole felt obliged to pull out when he was offered another job with a real fee attached.

His replacement was up-and-coming young director Toby Gough, whom Kit had found going walkabout in the Australian outback. Gough had been responsible for a groundbreaking *Julius Caesar* at the Edinburgh Festival, set against a Malawian background. It was also Kit who suggested Kylie for the leading ingénue role of Miranda. Toyah Wilcox had done it, so why not Kylie?

There would even be music. Kit had decided the play was to be reworked as a celebratory masque – which provided an excuse for a trio of Barbadian composers to rewrite 'Where the Bee Sucks' as a romping reggae-ska number, and turn some of the dialogue into calypsos and carnival songs.

Kylie found herself performing alongside some eminent thespians. David Calder, a distinguished actor who had just finished playing Miranda's father Prospero for the Royal Shakespeare Company, joined the cast to reprise the role. Jack Davenport from the cult television drama series *This Life* was also recruited; so was Roger Lloyd Pack, versatile veteran of top-rated television comedies such as *Only Fools and Horses* and *The Vicar of Dibley*, with whom some tabloids ludicrously suggested Kylie had enjoyed a fling.

The performance took place on 13 March. Kylie, clad in tattered rags and a few scraps of coral, stole what was left of the show when the kids had finished with it. As Shakespeare put it, the isle was full of noises – but Kylie's singing voice was not one of them. A solo had been written especially for her, but this was an acting job, and MusicKylie opted only to join her stage lover

Ferdinand (Rupert Penry Jones) briefly in a duet – and then merely to support his rather weaker vocal skills rather than to show off her own. Cast, audience and critics alike were in total accord: *The Tempest* was a triumph.

By the end of the month, Kylie's management had again been working on her behalf, and serious discussions with three major record companies were under way. She had already recorded a duet, 'In Denial', with Neil Tennant for the new Pet Shop Boys album. The track featured Tennant as a gay man singing an explanation of his life to Kylie, his daughter. Response to the track was, not surprisingly, overwhelming from the gay community and it was then that a single release was considered. The Pet Shop Boys were even approached to produce half of Kylie's upcoming album, but other commitments prevented that happening, much to their disappointment.

Kylie had also been visiting Peter Gabriel's Real World studios once again, this time to cut self-penned demos with Steve Anderson. Rumours of Kylie's loss of musical credibility had, as usual, been greatly exaggerated.

Shortly after this, another outbreak of unwanted press attention seemed to be unfolding. First with Jason Donovan, who had gone public six years previously about the nature of his four-year puppy-love relationship with Kylie, now reiterating his claim, adding that he had been Kylie's first lover.

Then in a bizarre attention-seeking bid, former prime minister of Australia Bob Hawke took part in a revealing documentary on the life of Michael Hutchence, and described how he watched while Kylie and Hutchence joined the Mile High Club by having sex on the seat of a Qantas jet. Kylie offered no explanation to either claim.

Two months later on her 31st birthday at the end of May, the Pet Shop Boys had persuaded her to opt for their record label, and a new recording contract with Parlophone had replaced the now defunct deConstruction deal. Kylie, of course, celebrated in style at London's prestigious Mayfair Hotel in London. Guests, including Prince Naseem Hamed, Robbie Williams, Baby Spice and Björk, partied well into the early hours – and Kylie kept up with her less vertically challenged chums in her usual pair of killer stiletto heels.

By June there were new rumours: Pete Waterman, no longer with partners Mike Stock and Matt Aitken, prematurely announced that he might be producing Kylie's new album. The deConstruction experiments had done wonders for her artistic reputation but nothing for her bank balance, and Parlophone wanted her to return to the tried and tested pop formula.

Even though Waterman was said to have been approached and seemed almost certain to accept, it was still early days. 'It's a very exciting prospect,' he told the *Sun* in June 1999. 'Kylie's doing an out-and-out pop album and I would have been surprised if they hadn't come to me. I would love to work with her again – she's the greatest artist I ever worked with. It would be great to try to recreate the fun and success we had.'

It was not to happen: although Kylie had decided on a return to pop because it's what she considered she does best, she was determined it would still be a progression, rather than returning to days gone by. If anything it was to be quality pop with an edge. And certainly that was what her new label had promised.

Meanwhile, the modelling experience she had gained at the London Fashion Week and for Hennes was put to charitable use later that summer. She was invited to walk the catwalk once again at a fashion show in Vienna, for the benefit of organisations which supported people with AIDS.

Statuesque diva Grace Jones was among the many guests, along with movie superstar Joan Collins. But true to form it was Kylie who raised eyebrows as well as cash by strutting her stuff in a black see-through number designed by Jeremy Scott.

The rest of the year was taken up with a mixture of work and play. A new album was under way: 'A bit of disco, some cheeky lyrics, but pretty much classic pop,' was how she described it. Now both Kylie and her new family, as she called them, at Parlophone were very exited about the new material she was recording. After all, there had never been any doubt that she could achieve commercial success again if marketed correctly.

But not even the far-sighted record company could have foreseen how the next couple of years would pan out. Least of all, Kylie herself.

# TWELVE

# RETURN TO GLORY

At the turn of the new millennium, Kylie, astonishingly enough, found herself to be more popular than ever before. And certainly with more panache than she had known since her early days with PWL. This time, however, if it was to work, it was to be strictly on her own terms.

Her new recording deal with Parlophone was just the ticket to start the ball rolling. It was something that had possibly been missing from other, earlier collaborations with record companies. Never before, for instance, had she received the kind of promotional support she was given over the next twelve months and still receives to this day. The same as any artist signed to a major label would expect.

Well aware of the changes that were now forced upon him, Terry Blamey had been on the lookout for a label ever since Kylie and deConstruction – the dance offshoot of BMG UK – had gone their separate ways, not for any reason other than the label was about to close its operation. Even though deConstruction still exists to this day, it is in name only, simply to issue some of their more credible and less commercial tracks. In fact, Kylie was one of the last artists to depart.

In some quarters it was said that she was dropped from the label, and had faced both public and industry humiliation, but nothing could be further from the truth. Why on earth would they want to let go of their most important signing? And again, why would she want to let go of them? Especially given that when it came to Kylie, what they did offer, more than any other label past or present, was a free artistic reign. For her and for her musical choices, right or wrong.

Although as gigantic as BMG, Parlophone, a subsidiary of EMI, and still 'the greatest recording organisation in the world', offered exactly what Blamey was looking for to re-establish Kylie's music career. They had the correct vision and marketing ploys to satisfy Blamey's demands. But was it still possible that Kylie could re-establish herself as the sassy pop princess who had grabbed 20 Top Ten hits, when deConstruction had been at a loss to know how to market her? It appeared that she could and –more importantly – so could Parlophone.

Even when she was told by the company's managing director that they didn't have anyone quite like her on their label, Kylie, exuding a mixture of confidence and shyness, replied, 'Nor does anyone else.'

And they wasted no time. In keeping with their promise to build upon Kylie's musical roots, they first needed to pitch her into the correct marketplace. But to do that successfully and without fear of critical retribution, they also needed quality song material. What could possibly be better than to commission some of the best songwriters in their field? Brian Rawlings, Johnny Douglas, Biff Stannard and Julian Gallagher (both best known for their work with the Spice Girls), Robbie Williams and his writing partner, Guy Chambers, would ultimately be the final choices from the cream of the current Tin Pan Alley.

In their bid to come up with what would best be described as the most perfect disco pop songs for her new album, no publishing company was left unturned, missed or overlooked. From the batch that was snapped up, one of those songs, sought and bought was 'Spinning Around'. And although then not an obvious first choice, in the end it proved to be the correct one to release as Kylie's debut single for her new label.

By the time the disc was at Number One, her first for over a decade, she was again in the news. Not this time for the controversial video that accompanied the track, considered by many to be one of the most sexually powerful by a female artist, but with a rumour of a new turn of events in Kylie's private life. Parlophone, on the lookout for greater exposure, weren't about to let the opportunity slip by.

The fact that she had been collaborating with Robbie Williams on the song 'Kids' was headline news and, as such, had the gossip columnists jumping up and down at the possibility of a romance between the two. As far as journalists were concerned, they couldn't go wrong. Kylie Minogue and Robbie Williams – it would be a relationship made in tabloid heaven.

It probably helped that soon after 'Kids' was released later that year, Williams had thrown himself into an ill-fated fling with Geri Halliwell before drifting away from it again. But since both had albums out at the time, one cannot help wondering if it was nothing more than a publicity drive to ensure that both parties received maximum exposure for their latest offerings. Surely, nothing could be better than to have your name and newest album splashed across the front of almost every magazine and national newspaper? It had worked before, so why not now, unless of course the rumours of love, tiffs and tears were, in fact, actually true. Either way, there is nothing quite like media exposure of a celebrity romance to ensure albums sell in their millions.

Assuming the idea of bringing Williams and his co-writer Guy Chambers into the Kylie picture was to offer up some new material for the album, and maybe a single or two, then again, it worked. Perhaps more so than anyone had expected.

'Kids', the first of those recorded, would indeed throw Kylie into a duet with Williams, and although the intention originally was to include the track only on the Williams album, it also turned up on Kylie's *Light Years* as well. More importantly, as far as Parlophone were concerned, it would provide Kylie with another Top Ten single, and a video that had most gasping for breath.

Not only that, but now working on the songwriting side of things as well, as she had done with others in the past, Kylie alongside Williams and Chambers came up with a couple of others, 'Loveboat' and 'Your Disco Needs You', that had equal potential. In fact it was the latter that had originally been planned as the first single to lift off the album. Released in both Germany and Australia, the track was strongly petitioned for UK release by Kylie's fans, and there was even talk at one point of picketing the London offices of EMI, the current home of Parlophone. But by that time, of course, the label, much to the fury and disappointment of the devotees, had already decided on 'Please Stay'. The video to go with it was another to be centred on sexy looks, style and dance routines, including one of Kylie sliding down a fireman's pole and another on top of a pool table. Even if they were becoming somewhat predictable by this time, even for Kylie herself – the treatment was still as stunning as ever.

With Kylie spending the Christmas vacation, as she had always done, in Australia with her parents, she had returned shortly after to her London home in Chelsea with renewed vigour and vitality. Terry Blamey noticed it as well. Quietly optimistic, he held no reservations about Kylie revitalising her recording career even further. He knew her too well, and his instincts always screamed approval of her foresight. And with the Parlophone deal now in place, he was even more convinced. Kylie, too, was equally enthusiastic about the possibility.

Even though she had probably earned more than a few million throughout her career, and money was probably never short, perhaps she was beginning to miss the adulation that she had known ever since she first bounced on to the small screen as perm-haired tomboy Charlene Mitchell, 14 years earlier.

With that knowledge, there came more. Unmarried and childless in her early 30s, and having lived with a girlfriend or two probably added to the pressure that she was now facing. Kylie may be a gay icon but when it came to her own sexuality that was a different matter altogether. People have inevitably asked, 'Is she gay herself, or bisexual?' The answer is definitely no, although rumours still crop up every now and then, and some have been quite strong on occasions.

Kylie has said that she had fancied other women, but hadn't done anything about it. She explained her position online at LiMBO, Kylie's most popular fansite. 'I think it's a natural part of being a woman to appreciate another woman's beauty and sexuality. I am attracted to other women and have affection and loving for them, and have been tempted, but the (good) boyfriends I've had have been enough to satisfy me.'

She was less reticent, of course, on recording her new album and on the subject of her successful re-emergence. Most monthly magazines though wouldn't be able to publish any feature or interview with her for at least another three months, the normal lead-times for most print media. With a new single already scheduled for June, it was clear to both Blamey and to Parlophone that there was little time to waste. Image-makers and stylists were hastily recruited for the onslaught that lay ahead.

One of those was photographer Vincent Peters.

Draped across a satin-sheeted divan in a Fulham studio, [wrote Justine Picardie when she caught up with her for a *Vogue* May 2001 feature] wearing very little indeed, she positively purrs for the camera, blonde hair tossed back to reveal come-to-bed eyes; glowing golden like a pint-sized Marilyn Monroe. Half an hour later, there's a short break in the proceedings while the lights are re-arranged. Kylie remains on the bed, alone for a moment, and closes her eyes. I go over to see if she'd like anything but when I get closer, I say nothing because she seems to be sleeping. Then all of a sudden she flicks open her pale blue eyes and I apologise for waking her.

But she wasn't asleep, just turned off.

It was a similar story elsewhere. Photo-shoot followed inter-view followed photo-shoot, each one appropriate to those now climbing over each other for Kylie to pose both on their front covers and inside. She was shot almost every way imaginable, from posing in little else other than twinkling fairy lights and her now trademark pout to being the girl-next-door. Most, though, showed her as a tanned, gorgeous, arching, foxy diva. In some she looked wise, in others innocent, carefree, glamorous, close-up, far away. In knickers, in cowboy boots, in more or less nothing.

Even though Kylie isn't shy about taking her clothes off and always wears stylish knickers from Gucci to Agent Provocateur, she was not very happy with the completed shoot – or rather the eventual fate of the pair of knickers that 'disappeared' from the cover of *GQ* magazine the previous year, as she told Frank Skinner on live television. 'I'm flipping through the magazine, and I was even a bit taken aback myself. It's one thing knowing what the picture is and then seeing it in front of you. And I get to this shot where they've obviously tampered with it. And I just said they've taken my knickers off. Oh, where did they go?'

In tribute to the famous 1970s Athena poster of a knickerless tennis player, the July cover of the men's glossy magazine featured a sizzling shot of Kylie hitching up her skirt on court and scratching her shapely bare bottom in front of a tennis net. Within hours of the magazine going on sale, media frenzy on the subject of nude bottoms and what some artists would do for publicity went into overdrive.

Within days, thousands of column inches were devoted to the pros and cons of nudity and more specifically to Kylie's bottom. If Blamey, Parlophone or Kylie's publicist had any concerns about the controversial cover, they were soon dispelled by the unprecedented public attention that the cover had attracted. If anything, it neatly promoted Kylie Minogue back into position as a name to be reckoned with.

The shot and others inside of Kylie without her knickers, including one of her completely naked with nothing more than a tennis racquet clasped over her breasts, earned *GQ* acres of free publicity and, with it, sent sales rocketing through the roof.

If Kylie's spokesperson answered the inevitable criticism with her claims that Kylie was only heralding the approach of Wimbledon, Kylie herself was much more adamant. As far as she was concerned, she had been wearing knickers throughout the shoot by Terry Richardson, the respected fashion photographer, and could not understand how *GQ* could simply airbrush them off her without first seeking her permission. 'I was a bit surprised that between the shoot and *GQ* appearing on the shelf, my knickers had got lost,' Kylie repeats.

Once again, the tabloids couldn't help but relish this and once again featured the shot of Kylie's pert posterior. Nevertheless, the argument continued.

Dylan Jones, editor of *GQ* was having none of it and vehemently denied Kylie's allegation. 'She always knew that this was the idea and that her knickers might fall off at the appropriate moment,' he said at the time. 'It is her bottom. We have not superimposed anyone else's. All the pictures were approved; she saw the pictures before publication. And it is great as bottoms go. It was, as Kenny Everett would have said, all done in the best possible taste.'

With Blamey's own goal of having complete copyright control over all Kylie's images, it is more likely that Kylie's management, if not herself, knew all about the removal of the offending knickers. Why shouldn't she? It goes without saying that both *GQ* and Kylie herself benefited enormously from the ensuing row.

In the same month that *GQ* hit the newsstands, the release of 'Spinning Around' was met with an equal amount of attention. Critical reaction was overwhelmingly positive: the track, although not revolutionary or unique, was still a beautifully crafted and superbly produced slice of pop disco music, the general consensus ran. But according to Kylie, the song 'just suited a full pop treatment. I'll just do what I feel sounds best. People read too much into things about what style is being sung. It's just music.'

All the same, the song provided Kylie with her fifth Number One in the UK, making her one of only two acts (the other is Madonna) to have had Number One hits in three consecutive decades from the Eighties to the present day.

As for the oft-described 'buttock bearing gold hot pants' she wore in the video that a girlfriend had picked up for only fifty pence from a market stall and Kylie had since filed away some place she couldn't quite remember, she cringes at the memory today.

'I often see something I've worn and just bury my head in my hands. I think I can cross the line sometimes, but I don't do it for cheap publicity. I had no idea that after the video came out the tabloids would be writing about my bum for a week. So I suppose I do regret some things – but react in the moment and often only realise the consequences later. You have to take chances with image.' Looking back over the years, she concludes, 'I have had some disasters but so has everyone.'

Public fascination with Kylie's hot pants should not have been that surprising. As *Sun* journalist Dominic Mohan, pointed out, 'It's the first time that an arse had got to Number One.' But it has also since proven characteristic of Kylie's favourite kind of video role, that of being sexually forthright. And today those are the words that best describe Kylie Minogue on video.

William Baker, Kylie's stylist and best friend for the last ten years, agrees. 'It's kind of a sexy song and we wanted like a clubby feel and those hot pants were just kind of perfect. And the video was like a showcase for Kylie's bum really.'

With her career now again on track, it wouldn't be long before Kylie was soon back to having someone new in her life – male model James Gooding. Although it would be at least another year before they decided to go public with the relationship, at the start it was never suggested, in some quarters, that the couple were anything more than friends. It was something Gooding would straighten out when he talked with London's *Evening Standard* magazine in December 2001.

Contrary to press speculation, 'We didn't meet at the Brit Awards,' he confirmed. 'We met in Los Angeles, at a party. The party was kind of boring, so we went out and got something to eat. When I met her, she was just finishing the album *Light Years* in LA and she was just this little, funny, geeky girl who I thought was really cute. We went out on a couple of dates and had fun. There was no pressure. And there was no pressure for a long while.' Even when he returned to London, there was still no pressure.

Eight years younger than Kylie, Gooding, despite the rumours of holding hands with old flame Sophie Dahl, kissing Beverley Bloom passionately on the way home from a theatrical fundraiser and proposing to Kylie after the couple were spotted shopping for rings, is still the perfect escort for her.

But Kylie simply balks at all the stories. 'I have to assume it's not true. I know how much is written about me and I think he's coping remarkably well with it because it must be the weirdest thing to suddenly be in this environment with all the rumours. I mean, no he didn't have posters of me on his wall; no we didn't have our first date at my house; no, we weren't shopping for rings.'

What actually happened, she continues, was 'We looked in that window because there were like three photographers down the street and they were pretty much just hounding us and so we almost weren't even looking.'

As for kissing Beverly Bloom, 'Oh I know what happened. It was a friend of his. I believe there were three of them in a cab and it was his friend who was getting quite friendly with a girl and I can only imagine that someone had said, "Oh, that's James Gooding over there," and someone thought ... I think it's just a case of mistaken identity. I know the girl they're talking about and no,' she laughs. 'He wouldn't have been kissing her.'

In the end, Kylie did her best to shrug off the attention. Besides, with Gooding, unreasonably handsome and good looking, his presence at public events, functions and ceremonies gave Kylie the support she had so long craved. More importantly, it put an end, once and for all, to the rumours about her own sexuality.

Adding fuel to the fire, however, Kylie, in reflective mood, was also debating, quite publicly, the issue over whether or not she thought she would ever have children of her own. At the age of 32, as most were quick to point out, her biological clock was well and truly clicking.

'I have come to realise I might well never be married and never have children,' she admitted. 'I look back on all those little girl things I used to say and it makes me laugh because, hey, here I am – still not married, still no kids. It doesn't upset me at all. It just looks like marriage and motherhood might not happen for me.

'I have some girlfriends who are lying about their age already, and it's all about the rings on fingers, settling down, the babies ... And I'm not like that. Maybe it's just because of my lifestyle. Or maybe it's because I don't think I'm as old as I really am.'

Whatever she thought, it was her stepping out with Gooding that attracted more attention than she, or probably Gooding, had in mind. More so than with any of her previous boyfriends for many years. All the same, it cannot be ignored that, out of bed, he also fulfilled another role. That of constant companion and escort. Dependable, reliable and trustworthy, it would possibly be true to say that it was a role that had been left somewhat vacant since her parting from Jason Donovan years earlier.

It wasn't all smooth sailing of course. On the final night of Kylie's UK tour he had left backstage without his VIP pass. On his return, none of the venue security team would let him back inside, even though, he persisted to snap, he was Kylie's boyfriend.

Kylie on the other hand was simply horrified. The man she had called her 'delightful scruff from Essex' had, it seemed, turned the situation into such an issue that in the process he also managed somehow to invite the interest of the media, who in turn dutifully captured the incident on film. It was almost like a fly-on-the-wall glimpse into Kylie's intensely private and secretive world. Now she would forever be asked the inevitable question, over and over, every time she gave an interview, 'What about James Gooding?'

Without shouting their business out loud, and taking one step at a time, Kylie and Gooding put their minds towards moving in together. They began shopping for a place in Shoreditch, East London. By February 2002 Gooding had found one, a canal-side luxurious two-bedroom loft apartment, converted from an old warehouse and which, although completely modernised, retained many of its original features such as timber floors, exposed brickwork and high ceilings.

Even so, there was still no talk of the couple tying the knot yet. 'We've laughed about marriage, but never talked about it seriously, ' Kylie confirmed. 'We've been though a lot together. James takes very good care of me and treats me like a princess.' But what most journalists really wanted to know, was whether the couple were finally planning to move in together?

After all, they had over the previous year been pictured literally everywhere they went in what was now becoming a constant intrusion by the tabloids. Everything from strolling arm-in-arm like an old married couple to hurtling around London on the micro scooters they had just got themselves.

Even with Kylie publicly linked to others over the years, and to some that she had never even met, what must have been a surprise to Gooding was when, some time earlier in their romance, she was quick to confirm that despite the attention, she had still not found her Mister Right. 'I'd like to be swept off my feet. I'm looking for a guy with humour and charisma and that's rare. I'd like him to be artistic, and I'd like a relationship that defies any description!

'I'm lucky because I've got such an exciting life. If I was home twiddling my thumbs all day, I might notice a gap. I firmly believe in fate and it's already written how long you are meant to be with someone. It's been so long since I had a relationship where I lived in the same town as my boyfriend that it would have its difficulties. I need my space.'

Not only that, she continues, but 'I've never been properly proposed to – that doesn't make me feel sad because normally I'm walking away from something, fear of commitment. I don't know if I'd marry. It's more important to be in a healthy relationship and I wouldn't have to be married to have a baby.'

Parlophone, however, were not concerned. They had something up their sleeve that would demonstrate just how impeccable Kylie's taste for the daring could be.

If the video for 'Spinning Around', with Kylie in her now legendary hot pants, had been seen as nothing more than a show-case for exposing more of her bum, then the promo for 'On A Night Like This' would put it firmly in the shade.

It would show Kylie as the bored wife of her millionaire husband (played by Rutger Hauer) climbing out of a swimming pool in wet clothes, erect nipples and breasts clearly visible through her now see-through clothing as she strips down to nothing other than knickers and diamonds in front of Hauer and his card-playing pals.

Perhaps what is not obvious is that she is the ghost of his wife, who has just killed herself and is floating dead in the pool. Now released from her past life, her spirit rises, free to dress up and go out gambling on the town, stroking her body, and return-ing at the end of the story to try and spook her lover by pushing over a glass vase, before again disappearing back into the pool. Her final resting place.

The video, despite its familiar sexual Kylie styling, and now with dark undertones added, seemed almost like a homage to one of her previous video characters, Eliza Day, in Nick Cave's 'Where The Wild Roses Grow' who also ended up her life float-ing dead in water.

Although the finished promo was said to have been re-shot to cut one scene of a completely naked Kylie standing in front of Hauer without knickers, nothing could be further from the truth. That was nothing more than a rumour that had been circulated by Parlophone to kick in a bizarre publicity drive. They were the first to spread gossip of a new censored version that had been made to ensure it got onto *Top of the Pops* and the like.

With or without the so-called offending sequences, now apparently toned down, it didn't really matter, because it made it onto most of the major pop shows anyway. But it also ended up as the most popular music video at that time to be lusted after by straight men despite Kylie's primarily gay audience. It also turned her into how she would be perceived from now on – one of the sexiest women on the planet and, maybe too, a fantasy figure for some lesbians. Something that Liam Gallagher, the other half of Oasis, would openly heckle her for at the Q Awards in London, with accusations that she was indeed gay herself.

But then again, Kylie loves to flirt. Whether with man, woman or as she once said, with a plain blank wall. It is probably why she is so good in all her music videos. Perhaps too, it is why her sexual prowess simply cascades out of her, quite naturally, whenever she performs. This was evident from the Agent Provocateur ad that she would shoot for a limited showing in London cinemas the following year.

It would show Kylie dressed in 'the world's most erotic lingerie' – a see-through bra and matching briefs, suspenders, stockings and stilettos – as she mounts and rides a red velvet-bucking bronco machine, all sexed up, as she puts it. The punch-line, observed *The Face* magazine, was that the men in the audience would be unable to stand afterwards on account of their erections. With Kylie decked out in such provocative attire, and doing what she was doing, it probably did that as well.

But after two days of filming the one-and-a-half minute footage in November 2001, she was horrified when she watched the first edit. 'I actually stopped breathing,' Kylie responded with her now familiar girl-next-door innocence. 'I thought, I hope my dad's not going to see this. It's such a fine line between looking cheap and just too full-on. I thought I've really outdone myself this time.' All the same, she continues, 'I was flattered when they asked me to do the ad and I loved doing it. It was sexy and lots of fun.'

It wouldn't be the first time that she had been fantasised about. According to *News of the World*, from a poll on the Internet, Kylie with Britney Spears was the top male fantasy for three-in-a-bed sex. Although Kylie did her best to shrug the attention off, the constant coverage did nothing more than make her laugh. That was the safest thing for her to do. 'I have to remove myself, detach myself, from that. It's a little weird. But with what I've been doing with the imagery and the videos and all of that, I couldn't have a turn about it.'

Alex James from Blur, however, could. He was another to confess to having been among all the other teenage boys who dream about her night after night. Robbie Williams, too, for that matter. He was equally enamoured after he had taped his duet with her at Masterock Studios, crowned later by what most called a sizzling performance on *Top of the Pops*.

They had recorded the routine several weeks earlier as Kylie would be out of the country when the single was released. And if the worse came to the worse, they could always fall back on the official video made to accompany the single even though it was considered a little on the provocative side. Probably for the sequence when both Kylie and Williams after kissing and caressing each other slip into a bath, stripped and naked, even though the audience sees nothing.

In fact, it was at the taping, just prior to their performance on *Top of the Pops* that Williams openly confessed that he had been dying to get his hands on Kylie for years. The feeling was mutual. 'I've heard that Robbie fancies me,' Kylie affirmed. 'He is so cute and immensely talented. He's funny, charming and he makes me laugh. When I worked with him, it was like putting two magnets together, there was a real electric charge between us.'

And nowhere was that better expressed than in their performance, confirmed one insider. 'There is clearly a [sexual] chemistry between them. It was the first time they ever performed the song together on stage, yet it was flawless. It was recorded in a single take in front of a live audience in Elstree Studios, and they [the audience] absolutely lapped it up.'

But within no time at all, Williams continued to promote his new album and Kylie did much the same with yet another whirl-wind round of promotional appearances and shows to support her own.

Among them was a live chat with BBC Online. It was where Kylie put herself in the hot seat to answer questions from fans and others. Although, the success of 'Spinning Around' had come as a total surprise to her, it was, she said, an absolutely delightful shock to enter at Number One.

But when asked what she was currently playing on her CD player, she explained, 'I've been listening to Coldplay, various club tracks from Ibiza and old hip-hop records. There's not much time in my schedule at the moment so I find I have to listen to different versions of my songs especially with the Olympics and Para-Olympics coming up.'

Regarding influences on her style, she was quick to reply. 'I couldn't choose one who's influenced me most. I take inspiration from fashion, films, music and friends. I think I'm a lot more knowing of my style than I have ever been before. It comes with age and maturity. That's not to say I won't be making any mistakes in the future. Sometimes I'm very much into fashion and other times, I wouldn't have a clue what's gong on.'

On the subject of being an icon, Kylie was more reticent.

'That's always a question that I find difficult to answer. I guess the easiest thing to say is that I'm very flattered and humbled. What I like about it is that it happened naturally. But believe me – it's not like that first thing in the morning when I shuffle to the kitchen and make my coffee.'

And why did she think she had become such a gay icon? She pondered for a while. 'It started a long time ago and I was the last person to know about it. I'm always hearing that I was aiming to capture the pink pound but what was happening when I heard that they were having a "Kylie" night every Sunday at the main gay pub in Oxford Street in Sydney. They sort of adopted me.

'I feel so supported by my gay audience, they've never let me down. I could go to war with them. I don't really think too much about what they like about me but there was a period after my first rush of success, when people turn against you. I was really being attacked in the press and my gay audience defended me. Perhaps they related to that.'

In the midst of this hectic round of interviews and photo-shoots, Kylie was about to take on the single most important date and possibly the biggest concert of her performance career, at the Olympic Games in Sydney. Resplendently dressed in pink show-girl attire and feathered head-dress and performing Abba's 'Dancing Queen' to over four billion people, it confirmed her transformation into the new Kylie Minogue.

She was carried on stage on a surfboard held by a gang of Australian football players, although she admits to being simply terrified in case they dropped her. 'But once I was on stage, it was unbelievable. It's very hard for me to convey what it was like. I felt like I was in the middle of some weird special effect where you're dragged into another dimension. There were drag queens everywhere, prawns on bicycles. Elle MacPherson walking out of this massive lens ... it was perfect. The whole stadium was dazzling!'

By the time you read this, Kylie will be in the throes of her huge stadium tour of the UK and Europe, and probably already feeling exhausted from the thought of facing her largest crowds ever during the 40 or so days and nights that she'll be on the road. Everywhere from her mother's old stomping ground in Cardiff to territories re-conquered in France, Italy and Spain.

Nonetheless she was very excited about the whole thing. 'The last tour represented *Light Years* and was very flamboyant, so this tour will be a representation of *Fever*. It's more streamlined, a little cooler in its presentation because the two albums are so different. The song I'm most excited about performing is "The Locomotion". We've worked out a sexed-up, funked-up Prince version of it, and it's fantastic.'

Equally fantastic was the global success of 'Can't Get You Out Of My Head'. So successful, in fact, that it raised the prospect of another assault on America in January 2002. That was when Kylie went on a ten-day promotional tour to Los Angeles and New York, appearing on the *Late Late Show* and *Jay Leno Show*, faced the usual solid rounds of magazine and newspaper interviews and took on an album signing at the Virgin Megastore in Times Square.

Breaking her fame in America wasn't as important now as it had been at the beginning of her career. 'It would have been many, many years ago,' she told Michael Parkinson, 'but for a long time now, it's just become lower and lower and lower on my list of priorities. You need to spend so much time in the States to get yourself known there. I couldn't spend a year – you know, "Kylie, Kaylie, Minouge, Minag, Minagwy. Oh! You're Australian, right." Frankly I'd rather put pins in my eyes for a year,' she laughs.

But, she continues, 'I always did say that – no disrespect to them at all – if I did have a song that started to take off, why it would be rude not to follow it up, so I did go to the States and we now have a Top Ten hit and who knows what's going to happen from here on.'

Even so, New York was where she would spend the most romantic weekend of her life with James Gooding. 'We just had had the day to ourselves, strolling around, hand-in-hand, having lunch, shopping in SoHo. It was perfect and made it all worthwhile – that's important to me – doing normal things and behaving like young lovers,' she told Dominic Mohan.

'It's bliss to do that and it means I can get back into work without the guilt. That means I can justify the hard work. I don't have a big entourage but there are always people around and it's nice to escape and have that freedom. I need that downtime – it's good and it makes my uptime great. I've always maintained that relationships are difficult anyway, whether you're jetting around the world or not.'

She didn't seem to have any qualms about growing up though. 'It's so nice to be well over 30 and still get treated like a little girl,' she confesses. 'I get away with murder because I'm always "sweet little Kylie". When I first came over to England, it was completely mad. I had a lot of success really quickly, but I was a bit too young to handle it. Now I'm older, I know what I'm doing and I'm loving it. Age has never been an issue with me. I don't feel old. I'm always treated like a little girl and I suppose I always feel very girly. People have never wanted me to grow up and I'm quite happy with them thinking of me like that.'

Soon after that weekend in New York, of course, she was crowned 'Queen of the Brits' when she walked away with two of the awards she was up for at the Brit Awards in London: Best

International Album for *Fever* and Best International Female Solo Artist. Not surprising really since she was the clear favourite in many people's eyes.

But it was her re-mixed performance of 'Can't Get You Out Of My Head' – dedicated to her father, Ron, still recovering from prostate cancer – that was the triumph of the evening at the event staged at Earls Court. Sliding out of an escalating giant CD with the now famous KYLIE logo spelt out in fluorescent red behind her, she was dressed in a white Dolce & Gabbana basque, silver boots just up over her knees and matching silver knickers as 'she writhed her way through her chart topper cleverly blended with New Order's dance classic "Blue Monday",' wrote Ben Todd in the *Daily Star*.

Her thoughts were never far away from her father, however. 'I love him so dearly,' Kylie said after winning her two first-ever Brit awards. 'He and Mum have been my rock throughout my life. He will be so proud of me. He will be the first person I call. I should really wait so I don't wake him up in the middle of the night – but he'll be so excited for me, I'm really proud.'

She was pleased with the outfit she had worn, apparently chosen out of 75 others. 'I thought it was sweet. It's totally white and I'm pretty much covered up, even though the dance routines were suggestive.'

But two days later, she was confessing to Davina McCall that she hadn't intended to show her knickers for the voyeuristic benefit of the cameras, nor perhaps as much cleavage as she did, even though they were, as McCall pointed out, 'the best boobs of the night'. But then again, Kylie would be prepared not to be surprised if her knickers adorned the front pages of the tabloids the next day. And needless to say, they did.

As for her breasts pushed up in a balconette-style bra, that was something that kept surprising her. 'I don't normally wear a bra like that,' Kylie insisted. 'I kept thinking: now don't go anywhere, stay where I put you. But I was a little nervous, more excited than nervous I have to say. [Now] I have Brits-lag! Not because I went out and had a huge night, but by the time I did get home, at around 2am, I couldn't sleep until about 4am.'

Kylie's appearance, suggestive or not, despite her dress rehearsal being a disaster when she got stuck on the giant CD in mid-air and was unable to move, resulted in a barrage of press coverage the following morning. With a look back at her career, Cristina Odone writing in the *Daily Mail* examined why she had become such a magnet for the men, the fans, the paparazzi and just about anyone with eyes in their heads.

Only Madonna – that other diminutive diva – can compare in terms of sheer eye-catching presence, but she just grabs our attention, while Kylie demands our affection, too. Millions of loyal fans turn her every single into a chart-topper, thousands of couples in Australia have named their daughter Kylie in tribute and her gay devotees have turned this supremely heterosexual vixen into a camp icon to rival Judy Garland.

But Kylie – through a process of endless reinventions that have seen her as a soap star in permed poodle's curls, a pop crooner boasting a No 1 hit, and a bronco-riding nude advertisement for a lingerie company – has ended up being much more: a singing sensation who flirts with porn, dangerous liaisons and scandalous behaviour, yet somehow manages to convey that what she really wants is a big hug from you.

And maybe that is the key to her success. That she has success-fully found a niche to slip into our hearts as someone who clev-erly blurs the boundaries between the feelgood girl and the come-to-bed temptress.

Whatever it is though, with another three music awards won in Britain and on the continent, a new single already pencilled in to follow 'Love At First Sight' and the Brits version of 'Can't Get You Out Of My Head', probably repeating the success of 'In Your Eyes', a new studio album, some tour dates in the US and perhaps a new long-overdue *Greatest Hits* compilation, an immediate future with Kylie Minogue sounds promising. Beyond that, of course, it's hard to know what she may do in the years to come.

One thing that seems certain is the break she'll most proba-bly take before thinking about recording anything new. Time off, she would say, to catch up with friends, family and boyfriend James Gooding. With renewed talk of marriage and maybe having children, even though by her own admittance she is no veteran to such proposals, it would also provide Kylie with the chance to take stock of her life once again.

# DISCOGRAPHY (UK)

*by Neil Rees*

## Singles

| Title (highest chart position) | Label | Date of release |
|---|---|---|
| I Should Be So Lucky (1) | PWL | Dec. 1987 |
| Got To Be Certain (2) | PWL | May 1988 |
| The Locomotion (2) | PWL | July 1988 |
| Je Ne Sais Pas Pourquoi (2) | PWL | Oct. 1988 |
| Especially For You (with Jason Donovan) (1) | PWL | Dec. 1988 |
| Hand On Your Heart (1) | PWL | Apr. 1989 |
| Wouldn't Change A Thing (2) | PWL | Apr. 1989 |
| Never Too Late (4) | PWL | Oct. 1989 |
| Tears On My Pillow (1) | PWL | Jan. 1990 |
| Better The Devil You Know (2) | PWL | May 1990 |
| Step Back In Time (4) | PWL | Oct. 1990 |
| What Do I Have To Do? (6) | PWL | Jan. 1991 |
| Shocked (DNA Mix) (6) | PWL | May 1991 |
| Word Is Out (16) | PWL | Sep. 1991 |
| If You Were With Me Now (with Keith Washington) (2) | PWL | Oct. 1991 |
| Keep On Pumpin' It (Visionmasters & Tony King featuring Kylie Minogue) (49) | PWL | Nov. 1991 |
| Give Me Just A Little More Time (2) | PWL | Jan. 1992 |

| | | |
|---|---|---|
| Finer Feelings (11) | PWL | Apr. 1992 |
| What Kind Of Fool (Heard All That Before) (14) | PWL | Aug. 1992 |
| Celebration (20) | PWL | Nov. 1992 |
| Confide In Me (2) | deConstruction/BMG | Sep. 1994 |
| Put Yourself In My Place (11) | deConstruction/BMG | Nov. 1994 |
| Where Is The Feeling? (Mixes) (16) | deConstruction/BMG | July 1995 |
| Where The Wild Roses Grow (with Nick Cave & The Bad Seeds feat. Kylie Minogue) (11) | Mute | Oct. 1995 |
| Some Kind Of Bliss (22) | deConstruction/BMG | Sep. 1997 |
| Did It Again (14) | deConstruction/BMG | Nov. 1997 |
| Breathe (14) | deConstruction/BMG | Mar. 1998 |
| GBI (German Bold Italic) (Towa Tei feat. Kylie Minogue) (63) | PWL | Oct. 1998 |
| Spinning Around (1) | Parlophone/EMI | June 2000 |
| On A Night Like This (2) | Parlophone/EMI | Sep. 2000 |
| Kids (With Robbie Williams) (2) | Chrysalis /EMI | Oct. 2000 |
| Please Stay (10) | Parlophone/EMI | Dec. 2000 |
| Can't Get You Out Of My Head (1) | Parlophone/EMI | Sep. 2001 |
| In Your Eyes (3) | Parlophone/EMI | Feb. 2002 |
| Love At First Sight | Parlophone/EMI | May 2002 |

## Other notable singles

| Title (highest chart position) | Label | Date of release |
|---|---|---|
| Locomotion (first single) (1: Australia) | Mushroom | May 1987 |
| Do They Know It's Christmas? (with Band Aid II) (1) | PWL | Dec. 1989 |
| Your Disco Needs You (Released in Germany and Australia: import available in UK (n/a) | EMI/FMR | 2001 |

## Albums

| Title (highest chart position) | Label | Date of release |
|---|---|---|
| Kylie (1) | PWL | July 1988 |
| Enjoy Yourself (1) | PWL | Oct. 1989 |
| Rhythm Of Love (plus Limited Edition 'Gold' Re-release) (9) | PWL | Nov. 1990 |
| Let's Get To It (15) | PWL | Oct. 1991 |
| Greatest Hits (1) | PWL | Aug. 1992 |
| Kylie Minogue (4) | deConstruction/BMG | Sep. 1994 |
| Kylie Minogue (originally titled: Impossible Princess) (10) | deConstruction/BMG | Mar. 1998 |
| Mixes (63) | deConstruction/BMG | July 1998 |
| Light Years (plus Limited Edition Remix Pack 2001) (2) | Parlophone/EMI | Sep. 2000 |
| Hits+ (41) | BMG | Oct. 2000 |
| Fever (1) | Parlophone/EMI | Oct. 2001 |
| Confide in Me (budget compilation) (n/a) | Camden/BMG | Nov. 2001 |

## Other notable albums

| Title | Label | Date of release |
|---|---|---|
| Kylie's Non-Stop History 50+1 (UK 'megamix' CD, originally released Japan 1992) | PWL | 1993 |
| Greatest Remix Hits Vol. 1 (Australian remix CD – import available in UK in 1998; also Japan 1993) | FMR | 1997 |
| Greatest Remix Hits Vol. 2 (Australian remix CD – import available in UK in 1998; also Japan 1993) | FMR | 1997 |
| Greatest Remix Hits Vol. 3 (Australian remix CD – import available in UK in 1998) | FMR | 1998 |
| Intimate & Live (Australian live CD – import available in UK in 1998) | FMR | 1998 |

# FILMOGRAPHY

## Television series

1980    *The Sullivans* – Kylie made her acting debut in this popular Word War II soap drama as Dutch orphan Carla in wartime Australia who befriends Australian troops. In later episodes which feature flashbacks of the character, Carla is played by sister Dannii.

1980    *Skyways* – Kylie and Jason Donovan play brother and sister in an episode of this short-lived children's drama set inside an airport, six years before they played lovers in *Neighbours*.

1984    *The Henderson Kids* – Kylie's first serious role as a tough-talking tomboy Char who is best friends with the female title character and with whom she helps to protect the cave she has inherited.

1985    *The Zoo Family* – Kylie is a battered child taken in by a zoo caretaker's family who causes havoc in her school holidays.

1985    *Fame and Fortune* – children's drama with Kylie as the loudmouthed sister of the main male character.

1986–8  *Neighbours* – Kylie in the role that made her a star, as motor mechanic Charlene Mitchell in the long-running soap drama about life on Ramsay Street.

1988    *The Comedy Company* – Kylie played Rebecca impersonating herself in this long-running series where many of Australia's finest comedians got their first big break nationally.

1994    *The Vicar of Dibley* – Kylie has a cameo role playing herself who appears out of nowhere to open the village Autumn Fayre in this episode ('Community Spirit') of the comedy series written by Richard Curtis and starring Dawn French.

1996    *Men Behaving Badly* – Kylie in another cameo role as herself, this time knocking on the door of Neil Morrisey and Martin Clunes in a Comic Relief special episode of the hilarious BBC series. The boys, both obsessed with Kylie, fail to recognise her!

## Feature films

1989    *The Delinquents* – directed by Chris Thomson. Kylie's first big screen role after *Neighbours*. She plays Lola Lovell in a Fifties love story, set in small-town Australia, who is madly in love with Charlie Schlatter, and fighting their parents to stay together despite both being under age.

1994    *Street Fighter* – directed by Steve E. de Souza. Kylie's first shot at an action movie alongside Jean Claude Van Damme as the hero of the popular video game, taking on a Russian general while trying to save the lives of the hostages held captive.

1995    *Hayride to Hell* – directed by Kimble Rendall. A short film in which Kylie plays a psychotic girl begging for the help of a salesman and then terrorising him during the ride home he has given her in his car.

1996    *Bio-Dome* – directed by Jason Bloom. Kylie plays a bio-scientist locked in an environmental bubble with Pauly Shore and Stephen Baldwin, after they have been dumped by their girlfriends, trying to prove themselves ecologically correct.

1996    *Misfit* – directed by Sam Taylor-Wood. Kylie is naked and miming to an ancient piece of opera in this short art film.

1997     *Diana and Me* – directed by David Parker. Kylie plays herself in a cameo role, being chased by paparazzi in a story that centres on Australian tourist Diana Spencer visiting London to meet her namesake.

2000     *Cut* – directed by Kimble Rendall. Kylie is a bitchy film director who gets murdered by having her tongue cut out in the opening sequences of this Australian horror movie.

2000     *Sample People* – directed by Clinton Smith. About a girl nightclub owner, played by Kylie, who becomes entangled in various scams involving money and drugs.

2001     *Moulin Rouge* – directed by Baz Luhrmann. Kylie has a cameo role as the Green Fairy who appears to Ewan McGregor after he downs some absinth in the fantastical underworld of Paris's legendary Moulin Rouge.

# SOURCES

## 1. Interviews

Kylie Minogue (1997) (1998 courtesy of Neil Rees)
Andrew Cowan-Martin
David Howells
Steve Anderson (courtesy of Neil Rees)
Will Baker (courtesy of Neil Rees)

## 2. Newspaper and magazine articles

*Attitude*
'The Show Pony', by Barbara Ellen, September 1997

*Australian Style*
'Kylie', by Sebastian Smee, 1998

*B Magazine*
'The Kylie Phenomenon', November 2001

*Daily Express*
'Exclusive', by Annie Leask, 15 August 1991

*Daily Mail*
'Kylie the Rebel Next Door', 20 May 1989
'Kylie, the Bad Girl in Black', 6 December 1989
'Cosy but Sexy, the Girl's Full of Surprises', by Cristina Odone,
    21 February 2002

*Daily Mirror*
'Stunner Kylie Goes It Alone', 6 December 1989
'From Carol O'Connor in Melbourne', 29 May 1989
'News Story', April 1989

*Daily Star*
'Kylie Moves into Julian's Love Nest', by Julia Kuttner,
    30 March 1994
'I Won It for Sick Daddy Says Kylie', by Ben Todd,
    21 February 2002

*ES Magazine*
'Hey, Good Looking', by Polly Vernon, 21 December 2001

*Esquire*
'You Should Be So Lucky', by Amy Raphael, October 1997

*The Face*
'Kylie 02: In with a Rocket', by Chris Heath, December 2001

*Follow Me* (Australia)
'Kylie Vamps Up', December 1990

*Gay Times*
'The Happy Kylie Show', by David Meech, July 1994

*Glasgow Evening News*
'Kylie's the Real Spin Doctor', by Fraser Middleton,
   3 March 2001

*GQ*
'At Your Service', July 2000

*Heat*
'Posh & Kylie Go Head to Head', 11 August 2001
'The Truth About My Men', by Andrew Lawton, 13 October 2001
The Heat Interview: Kylie Minogue', by Simon Gage,
   22 December 2001
'Brits Awards 2002: Backstage with the Celebs', 2 March 2002

*Hello*
'Kylie Minogue', by Stuart Husband, 5 March 2002

*ID*
'Kylie – The Making of a Pop Goddess', by John Godfrey,
   July 1994
'Pop Love, Kylie!', by Mandi James, 1991

*Ministry*
'Saucy Minx', by Pearly, April 1998

*More*
'Special K', by Helen Bazuaye, 19 September 2001

*News Letter*
'Kylie's Image Is Firmly Behind Her', by Paul Martin,
   2 March 2001

*Night & Day*
'She Should Be So Lucky', by Vincent Lovegrove, 18 April 1999

*NME*
'A Wallaby Together', by Derek Ridgers, September 1994

*Now Starstyle*
'Pop's Hottest Style Icon', by Rebecca Fletcher, Winter 2001

*Now*
'Even Madonna Thinks I'm Cool', by Clare Alexander,
   6 March 2002

*Q Magazine*
'Cash For Questions', by Kerry Potter, April 2001

*Satellite TV Europe*
'Woman of the Year', cover feature, February 2002

*She*
'What Kylie Did Next', July 2000

*Sky*
'Kylie Bloody Minogue', October 2000

*Smash Hits*
'Michael In His Own Words', by Jaynie Senior, 1990

*Sun*
'Kylie Flees Mob', by Dina Malik, 4 April 1988
'Security Men Grab Kylie's Handcuffs', by Paul Hooper,
    9 September 1991
'Re-Pete Performance', 12 June 1999
'Geri 'n' Kylie's TFI Kiss', 25 October 1999
'I Just Had the Most Romantic Weekend of My Life, Says Kylie',
    by Dominic Mohan, 20 February 2002

*Today*
'Exclusive', by Lester Middlehurst, 8 December 1989

*Vogue*
'Pop's Pocket Venus', June 2001

*Womans Day* (Australia)
'Kylie's Crusade for Kids', November 1998


**3. Television and radio**

*An Audience With Kylie Minogue*, ITV, October 2001
*The Brits 2002*, ITV, February 2002
*Interview with Richard Wilkins: Witness*, Australia Channel 9,
    1997
*Interview with Davina McCall*, Capitol FM, February 2000
*Kylie Liquid News Special*, BBC Choice, 15 February 2002
*Parkinson*, BBC 1, 23 February 2002
*Planet Rock Profiles*, ITV, December 2001
*The Story of Kylie*, MTV, January 2001
*Today*, Australia Channel 10, 1998
*Top 10 Princesses of Pop*, Channel 4, December 2001

## 4. Video

In addition to the movies listed in the filmography we screened many videos including:

> *Greatest Video Hits*
> *Intimate and Live*
> *Kylie Live*
> *The Kylie Tapes 94–98*
> *Live in Sydney*

and selected promos, enhanced videos and appearances on

> *CD:UK*
> *The Frank Skinner Show*
> *TFI Friday*
> *Top of The Pops*

## 5. Cinema (London)

Agent Provocateur (commercial), limited screenings, December 2001

## 6. Books

*The Official Kylie Minogue Annual* (1990) World International
    Publishing
Scatena, D. (1997) *Kylie: An Unauthorised Biography*. Penguin
    Books

Rees, D. and Crampton, L. (1994) *The Guinness Book of Rock Stars* (3rd edn). Guinness Publishing


**7. Internet**


Dot Music (http://www.dotmusic.com)

Internet Movie Database (http://us.imdb.com)

LiMBO Kylie Minogue Online (http://www.kylie.co.uk)

Kylie Fever (http://www.kyliefever.com)

The Official Kylie Minogue Website (http://www.kylie.com)